America's National Parks

EVERGLADES
NATIONAL PARK

Adventure, Explore, Discover

SUSAN JANKOWSKI

MyReportLinks.com Books
an imprint of

Enslow Publishers, Inc.
Box 398, 40 Industrial Road
Berkeley Heights, NJ 07922
USA

MyReportLinks.com Books, an imprint of Enslow Publishers, Inc. MyReportLinks®
is a registered trademark of Enslow Publishers, Inc.

Library of Congress Cataloging-in-Publication Data

Jankowski, Susan.
   Everglades National Park : adventure, explore, discover / Susan Jankowski.
      p. cm. — (America's national parks)
   Includes bibliographical references and index.
   Summary: "A virtual tour of Everglades National Park, with chapters devoted to the history of
this Florida region, history of the park, plant and animal life, environmental problems facing the
park, and activities in the area"—Provided by publisher.
   ISBN-13: 978-1-59845-091-0 (hardcover)
   ISBN-10: 1-59845-091-3 (hardcover)
   1. Everglades National Park (Fla.)—Juvenile literature. 2. Natural history—Florida—Everglades
National Park—Juvenile literature. 3. Everglades (Fla.)—History—Juvenile literature. 4. Natural
history—Florida—Everglades—Juvenile literature. I. Title.

   F317.E9J26 2008
   975.9'39—dc22

                            2007038262

Printed in the United States of America

10 9 8 7 6 5 4 3 2 1

To Our Readers:
Through the purchase of this book, you and your library gain access to the Report Links that specifically back up this book.
The Publisher will provide access to the Report Links that back up this book and will keep these Report Links up to date on
www.myreportlinks.com for five years from the book's first publication date.
We have done our best to make sure all Internet addresses in this book were active and appropriate when we went to press. However,
the author and the Publisher have no control over, and assume no liability for, the material available on those Internet sites or on
other Web sites they may link to.
The usage of the MyReportLinks.com Books Web site is subject to the terms and conditions stated on the Usage Policy Statement on
www.myreportlinks.com.
A password may be required to access the Report Links that back up this book. The password is found on the bottom of page 4 of
this book.
Any comments or suggestions can be sent by e-mail to comments@myreportlinks.com or to the address on the back cover.

♻ Enslow Publishers, Inc., is committed to printing our books on recycled paper. The paper in every book contains 10% to 30%
post-consumer waste (PCW). The cover board on the outside of each book contains 100% PCW. Our goal is to do our part to help
young people and the environment too!

Photo Credits: AP/Wide World Photos (Ray Fairall), pp. 94–95; APN Media, p. 12; Audubon of Florida, p. 60;
Comprehensive Everglades Restoration Plan, p. 91; © Corel Corporation: pp. 3, 6 (top banner), 23, 63, 74;
Defenders of Wildlife, p. 86; Ecological Society of America, p. 106; Enslow Publishers, Inc., p. 34; Florida Exotic Pest
Plant Council, p. 83; Florida International University Libraries, p. 29; Florida Museum of Natural History, p. 84;
© Frank Steele, p. 28; Friends of the Everglades, p. 56; Historical Museum of Southern Florida, p. 113;
istockphoto.com, pp. 1 (inset photo–Kevin Thomas), 6 (wetlands) & 26–27 (Chloe Beaufreton), 7 & 98 (kayak/Vittorio
Sciosia), 110–111 (CJ McKendry); Henry Morrison Flagler Museum, p. 49; johnhorse.com, p. 24; Library of
Congress, pp. 20, 37, 42, 52; MyReportLinks.com Books, p. 4; NASI, p. 57; National Park Service/Enslow Publishers,
Inc., p. 5; National Park Service, pp. 18, 58–59 (Rodney Cammauf), 87; National Parks Conservation Association,
p. 114; National Wildlife Federation, p. 101; The Nature Conservancy, p. 64; shutterstock.com, pp. 1 (background
photo–Tomasz Szymanski), 6 (heron & roseate spoonbills), 7 (gator & visitor center), 8–9, & 10 (FloridaStock), 15
(Rob Ahrens), 26–27 (laptop), 30 (FloridaStock), 54 (Jeff Gynane), 58–59 (camcorder), 62 (FloridaStock), 65
(PSHAW–PHOTO), 68 (Christopher Meder), 98–99 (iPod), 103 (Wayne Johnson), 104–105 (Peter Brett Charlton);
slaveryinamerica.org, p. 40; South Florida Water Management District, p. 88; State Archives of Florida, pp. 46–47,
51; State Library and Archives of Florida, p. 21; State of Florida, p. 90; theevergladesstory.org, p. 32; University of
Florida, pp. 66, 72; University of Virginia, Miller Center of Public Affairs, p. 39; U.S. Department of Agriculture,
p. 80–81, 82; U.S. Fish and Wildlife Service, p. 71, 76–77; Wheeling Jesuit University, Center for Educational
Technologies, p. 14; wikipedia.org (Marc Averette), p. 102; World Wildlife Fund, p. 69.

Cover Photo & Description: Inset photo: istockphoto.com (Kevin Thomas/egret in flight, Everglades National
Park); background: shutterstock.com (Tomasz Szymanski)

CONTENTS

MyReportLinks.com Books
Great Books, Great Links, Great for Research!

The Internet sites featured in this book can save you hours of research time. These Internet sites—we call them **"Report Links"**—are constantly changing, but we keep them up to date on our Web site.

When you see this "Approved Web Site" logo, you will know that we are directing you to a great Internet site that will help you with your research.

Give it a try! Type http://www.myreportlinks.com into your browser, click on the series title and enter the password, then click on the book title, and scroll down to the Report Links listed for this book.

The Report Links will bring you to great source documents, photographs, and illustrations. MyReportLinks.com Books save you time, feature Report Links that are kept up to date, and make report writing easier than ever! A complete listing of the Report Links can be found on pages 116–117 at the back of the book.

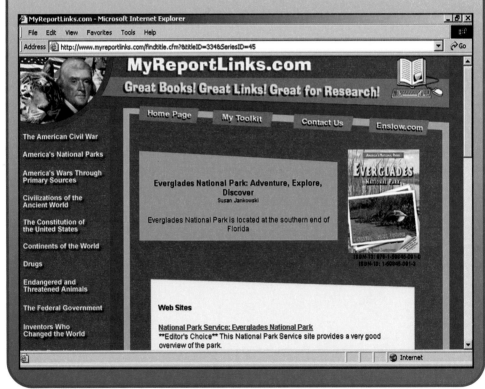

Please see "To Our Readers" on the copyright page for important information about this book, the MyReportLinks.com Web site, and the Report Links that back up this book.

Please enter **ENP1536** if asked for a password.

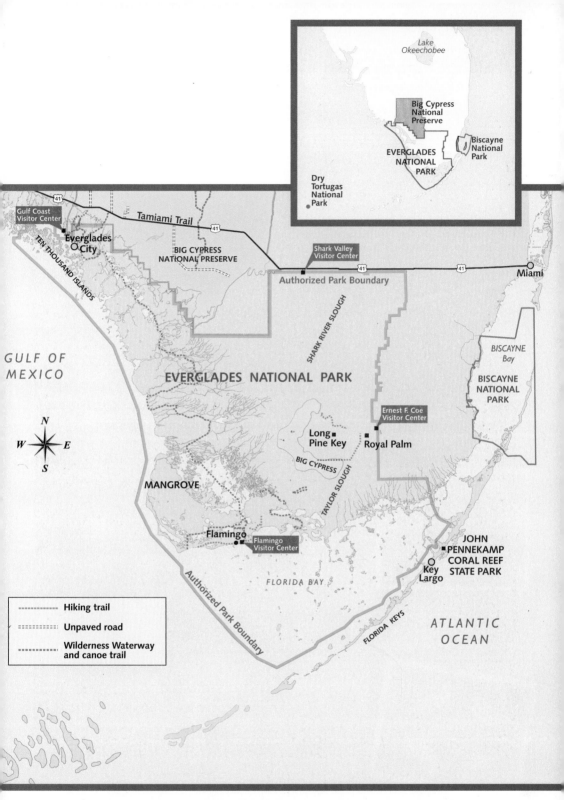

Lake
Okeechobee

Big Cypress
National
Preserve

Biscayne
National
Park

EVERGLADES
NATIONAL
PARK

Dry
Tortugas
National
Park

Gulf Coast
Visitor Center

Everglades
City

TEN THOUSAND ISLANDS

Tamiami Trail

BIG CYPRESS
NATIONAL PRESERVE

Shark Valley
Visitor Center

Authorized Park Boundary

Miami

SHARK RIVER SLOUGH

GULF OF
MEXICO

EVERGLADES NATIONAL PARK

BISCAYNE
Bay

BISCAYNE
NATIONAL
PARK

Ernest F. Coe
Visitor Center

Long
Pine Key

Royal Palm

N
W   E
S

BIG CYPRESS

TAYLOR SLOUGH

MANGROVE

Flamingo

Flamingo
Visitor Center

JOHN
PENNEKAMP
CORAL REEF
STATE PARK

Key
Largo

Authorized Park Boundary

FLORIDA BAY

FLORIDA KEYS

ATLANTIC
OCEAN

- - - - - - - Hiking trail

- - - - - - - Unpaved road

- - - - - - - Wilderness Waterway
and canoe trail

▲ Located at the southern tip of Florida, southwest of Miami, Everglades
National Park covers more than 1.5 million acres. See an additional
map on page 34 for more details.

- Everglades National Park holds many international titles. Across the world, it is seen as a special place that is important to the earth's environment.

- The Everglades is the largest subtropical wilderness in the United States.

- The Everglades ecosystem begins at Turkey Lake in central Florida and includes the freshwater of Lake Okeechobee in south central Florida. It is one of America's largest freshwater lakes.

- People who live in Florida call this area "the Glades."

- Most of the backcountry campsites in Everglades National Park can only be reached by water. All require a permit.

- Visitors often travel through the park by kayak or canoe. Airboats are not permitted in Everglades National Park (except for use by those with research permits), but airboat tours of nearby areas are available through private operations. Deeper water boat and tram tours are offered at several locations in the park.

- Ten Thousand Islands is an area in the park that is a maze of water and mangrove trees. It is part of the largest mangrove forest in the United States.

- The open waters of the mangrove forests and the Florida Bay make up one-third of Everglades National Park.

- The Everglades is home to endangered species such as the Florida panther and the West Indian manatee.

- Each year, fifteen thousand of the more than 1 million people who visit Everglades National Park are students.

- A century ago, settlers viewed the Everglades as worthless swampland. They began draining it to water crops on farms and for the construction of housing developments.

- Today, the Everglades is less than half the size of its original 11,000 square miles (28,490 square kilometers).

- Small islands called hammocks rise above the saw grass. They are dry places for trees, plants, and animals.

- Florida's Seminole Indians fled deep into the Everglades in the 1800s to hide from U.S. soldiers. They were never caught.

- Local American Indians, such as the Seminoles, host alligator wrestling shows near the park.

- In the nineteenth century, American settlers of the Everglades traded vegetables, sugarcane syrup, and fish for supplies shipped from Key West, Fort Myers, and later, Tampa, Florida.

- The algae plant forms a layer over the shallow water of Everglades wetlands. It acts as a filter and is food for animals.

- Each year, Everglades National Park staff works to protect and repair parts of the park that are damaged by hurricanes.

- The park's "mosquito season" is the same as its rainy season, which is May through October or November.

- Lightning strikes often start fires in Everglades National Park. They are usually allowed to burn, but are controlled if they become a threat to special habitats or humans. Fires and storms are considered to be good for the Everglades.

- Many animals are killed by car accidents on roads in Everglades National Park each year. Even alligators are known to cross roads.

- "No Wake Zones" signs are posted in waterways to prevent boaters from running over manatees that live in or near the park.

- Scientists know how to check color patterns on snakes in the Everglades to see whether they are poisonous. But for most people, it is difficult to tell the difference between those that are poisonous and those that are not. It is best to avoid wild snakes in the park.

- Coral reef gardens surround Everglades National Park and the south Florida coastline.

- Coral takes centuries to grow.

Chapter 1

Dawn breaks over the Everglades.

World-Famous "River of Grass"

t is daybreak and a blazing red ball of fire is rising in the sky. The silence is broken by the lone call of a bald eagle to its mate. It snatches a fish from a shallow lake surrounded by mud and saw grass. Even the frogs are quieting down as the stars fade.

Then there is no sound—just stillness—before the sun bursts over the water to reflect its hot, white light. It is a new day in Everglades National Park.

The weather is humid and hot. Already the temperature is a steamy 80 degrees Fahrenheit (about 27 degrees Celsius). This afternoon, lightning will strike somewhere in the park and start a brush fire. This is natural in "the Glades," as people in Florida call the area. This state has more lightning strikes than anywhere else in the United States.[1]

Lightning fires can burn trees in rocky pine forests, as well as cypress trees, saw grass, and cabbage palms on hammocks. These are shady islands covered with brush that rise out of the river of grass. The hammocks give protection to many animals. Yet fires can be good for the Everglades, too. They clear out old brush so new plants can have room to grow. Firefighters, scientists, engineers, and park rangers strive to control the spread of fire. These are some of the people working to save the plants and animals across Florida and in its parks.

▼ The great blue heron, a common wading bird in the Everglades, can grow to be over four feet tall.

⊛CRAWLING WITH CREATURES

Lightning can cause a Florida panther to take cover on a hammock. The big cat could miss its chance to catch a white-tailed deer as it darts into a stand of pines. But like many animals that live in Everglades National Park, the panther can survive a storm and the resulting downpour of rain that follows. The Everglades receives about sixty inches (one hundred fifty centimeters) of rainfall each year.

Colorful wading birds like the roseate spoonbill, white egret, and great blue heron will also likely survive the storm. Manatees glide through the park's Florida Bay in search of sea grass. During harsh weather, manatees can dive underwater or swim to wherever it is calm and warm. They may cross a dolphin in their path that has come inland from the ocean. Or, when heading out to sea, manatees may swim past sea turtles, sharks, or schools of fish.

Lurking among these creatures are alligators and crocodiles. The Everglades is one of the few places in the world that is home to both species. In the Everglades wetlands, alligators and crocodiles eat fish, frogs, ducks, or other animals in or near the water. These large reptiles are related to dinosaurs that roamed the earth millions of years ago.[2] Alligators live in the freshwater areas of the park, while crocodiles live in the saltwater, or "brackish" waters. Seldom do these reptiles live in the same areas.

The mud of the Everglades is crawling with life. Spiders as big as a human hand creep along mangrove tree roots above this mud, or skim the tops of plants. In the Everglades, everything is moving. Everything is alive!

All of this movement takes place among the bright colors of flowers that soak up the rain and sunshine. These include lilies, orchids, and other blooms.

Large animals prowl in the shade of bald cypress, mangrove, oak, palm, and pine trees. Everglades National Park is home to more than a

Oh, Ranger!: Everglades National Park offers an online tour. It includes information about the park's plants, wildlife, and history as well as conservation concerns. Visitor information and an article on the preservation of the Everglades are also provided.

dozen endangered species.[3] More information on these plants and animals can be found on the National Park Service Web site about this park. Today, the protection of endangered species in the Everglades and across America is the law.

Pioneers who settled Florida began draining water from the Everglades at the turn of the twentieth century. This destroyed habitat for many animals. Over the next few decades, cities like Miami grew. But the growth of cities also took away land from Everglades's animals. For example, the number of wading birds nesting in colonies here has dropped by over 90 percent since the 1930s.[4]

HAZARDOUS ROAD CROSSINGS

One modern threat to animals is cars on the roads through the park. Many animals are accidentally hit by cars in the Everglades.[5] "Wildlife Crossing" signs alert drivers as they travel through places where there are deer, bear, and panthers. Speed limits are posted and enforced. At visitor centers, park staff can offer tips on what to watch out for on the road.

One third of Everglades National Park is open water. People can only get to many places in the park by canoe, kayak, or small boat. The Everglades begins with waters flowing down from Lake Okeechobee north of the park. It is one of the

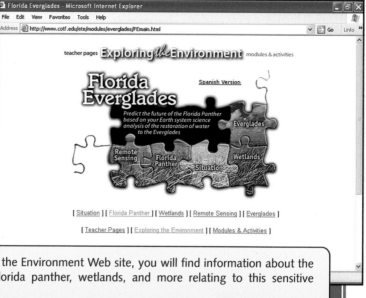

teacher pages **Exploring** *the* **Environment** modules & activities

Florida Everglades

Spanish Version

Predict the future of the Florida Panther
based on your Earth system science
analysis of the restoration of water
to the Everglades

Everglades

Remote
Sensing

Florida
Panther

Situation

Wetlands

[Situation] [Florida Panther] [Wetlands] [Remote Sensing] [Everglades]

[Teacher Pages] [Exploring the Environment] [Modules & Activities]

Exploring the Environment: Florida Everglades

On this Exploring the Environment Web site, you will find information about the Everglades, the Florida panther, wetlands, and more relating to this sensitive ecosystem.

Access this Web site from http://www.myreportlinks.com

largest freshwater lakes in the United States. Yet at its deepest point, Lake Okeechobee is only thirteen feet (four meters) deep, and its average depth is about ten feet (three meters).

Only researchers with special permits are allowed to use airboats within the borders of Everglades National Park. But airboats are often used for travel on Lake Okeechobee, or in the Big Cypress National Preserve and area wetlands. The roar of airboat engines can be loud, and riders often wear headgear to muffle this sound.

The lake is also a favorite spot for freshwater sportfishing. The U.S. and state governments post seasons for catching many species. Florida's fresh

NEXT 2 MILES

This sign helps to alert drivers in the area to the presence of panthers. The panther is Florida's state animal.

and salty waters are home to fish such as bass, bluefish, bream, catfish, crappie, gar, grouper, mackerel, marlin, mullet, pompano, red snapper, sailfish, sea trout, shark, shrimp, and tarpon. Shellfish such as clam, conch, oyster, and scallop also live in the waters along Florida's shores.

THE SUN'S POWERFUL RAYS

South Florida is fairly close to the earth's equator. This is the part of Earth that is right in the path of the sun's rays. A person with unprotected skin can get a sunburn in Florida in just a few hours (or less). It is important for people and animals to protect themselves from the sun's ultraviolet rays. This is especially true in the middle of the day when the sunshine is strongest.

Cattle ranchers in south central Florida protect themselves from the power of the sunshine. They wear hats, sunglasses, pants, and shirts with long sleeves. They also know to step carefully in the Everglades. Over two dozen species of snakes live in this ecosystem. Four inject poison with their bite. Farmers and citrus and sugarcane workers in the fields are always on the lookout for snakes while they tend their crops. It is common for people who live in the Everglades to wear tall "snake boots" to protect their feet and legs while walking outside.

Central and south Florida are known for their orange and grapefruit groves. Bees make honey from orange blossoms, which give off a sweet scent like perfume. They buzz back and forth to their hives among azalea, gardenia, hibiscus, jasmine, oleander flowers, and dogwood blooms. At the start or end of a long day, a cool drink of fresh fruit juice on ice is most welcome. Florida farmers grow strawberries and other fruits and vegetables, too. Sugarcane is also a big crop for some of Florida's farmers.

The number of mosquitoes in the Everglades rises with the yearly rainfall during summer months. During "hurricane season," which officially runs from June 1 to the end of November, strong hurricane winds of more than 100 miles (160.9 kilometers) per hour can hit sections of the park. In the late summer and fall of 2005, Hurricanes Katrina and Wilma resulted in a forced closure of parts of Everglades National Park. Staff worked to restore parts of the park and repair the hurricanes' damage to man-made structures.[6]

⇒ An Environmental Engine

Stormy weather, insects, and dinosaur-like creatures do not keep tourists away from the Everglades. More than a million people visit Everglades National Park each year. One quarter of these visitors come from other states and countries. They arrive wearing hats, sunscreen lotion, and insect repellent to explore the only subtropical preserve in North America.

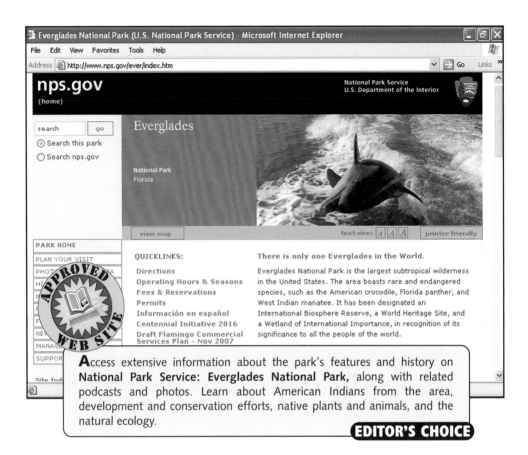

Everglades National Park (U.S. National Park Service) - Microsoft Internet Explorer

File Edit View Favorites Tools Help

Address http://www.nps.gov/ever/index.htm   Go   Links »

nps.gov
(home)

National Park Service
U.S. Department of the Interior

search   go
⦿ Search this park
◯ Search nps.gov

Everglades

National Park
Florida

view map   text size: A A A   printer friendly

PARK HOME
PLAN YOUR VISIT
PHOT...
HI...
M...
F...
NE...
MANAG...
SUPPOR...
Site Ind...

QUICKLINKS:

Directions
Operating Hours & Seasons
Fees & Reservations
Permits
Información en español
Centennial Initiative 2016
Draft Flamingo Commercial
Services Plan - Nov 2007

There is only one Everglades in the World.

Everglades National Park is the largest subtropical wilderness in the United States. The area boasts rare and endangered species, such as the American crocodile, Florida panther, and West Indian manatee. It has been designated an International Biosphere Reserve, a World Heritage Site, and a Wetland of International Importance, in recognition of its significance to all the people of the world.

Access extensive information about the park's features and history on **National Park Service: Everglades National Park,** along with related podcasts and photos. Learn about American Indians from the area, development and conservation efforts, native plants and animals, and the natural ecology.

EDITOR'S CHOICE

Some people say the Everglades looks something like "Jurassic Park," which is the setting for a famous book by author Michael Crichton.[7] (The story later became a popular film series directed by Steven Spielberg and produced by Universal Pictures.) The pterodactyl-like birds flying overhead, reptiles lurking below, and bushy, tropical plants make it easy to understand why people would say this.

Thousands of park visitors each year are students. To help them plan their visit, the U.S. National

Park Service offers a virtual tour of Everglades National Park on its Web site.

Today, Everglades National Park is world famous. People across the globe value this special place and its diverse plant and animal species. Most important is the environmental "engine" that the Everglades creates. The water of this ecosystem drives life cycles throughout the region. Its plants put oxygen back into the air. Its ecosystem is even linked to the weather. For this reason, the park is officially seen as a special place by the United Nations and other international organizations. These groups named the Everglades an International Biosphere Reserve, a World Heritage site, and a Wetland of International Importance.

⊜ DRAINING THE GLADES

Because of all of this attention, it is hard to imagine that a century ago people saw the Everglades as a worthless swamp. In the early 1900s, the U.S. Army Corps of Engineers drained water from the Everglades for use by farmers. This allowed them to grow sugarcane, citrus fruits, and other crops. It made it possible for people in nearby towns to build houses, stores, hospitals, and schools.

Then a book entitled *The Everglades: River of Grass,* written by author and crusader Marjory Stoneman Douglas, was published in 1947. In this classic work, Marjory Stoneman Douglas wrote about the wild beauty of the Everglades and how it keeps the environment in its natural balance. She warned that draining water from the Everglades would destroy life both inside and outside its special ecosystem.

Marjory Stoneman Douglas understood that the life in south Florida depends on the evaporation of

This photo shows efforts to dredge the Miami Canal in order to drain the Everglades.

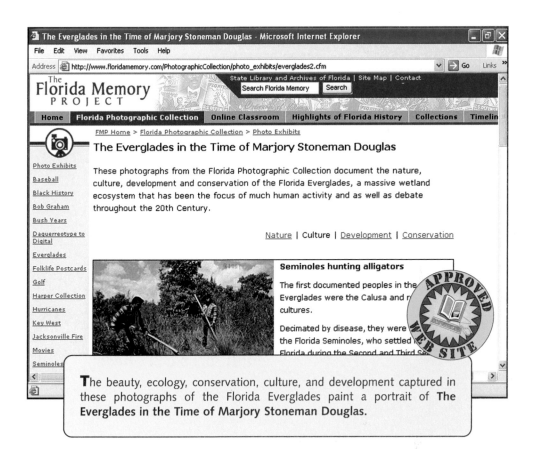

The Everglades in the Time of Marjory Stoneman Douglas - Microsoft Internet Explorer

File   Edit   View   Favorites   Tools   Help

Address   http://www.floridamemory.com/PhotographicCollection/photo_exhibits/everglades2.cfm   Go   Links »

The **Florida Memory** P R O J E C T

State Library and Archives of Florida | Site Map | Contact

Search Florida Memory   [Search]

Home | **Florida Photographic Collection** | Online Classroom | Highlights of Florida History | Collections | Timelin

FMP Home > Florida Photographic Collection > Photo Exhibits

The Everglades in the Time of Marjory Stoneman Douglas

Photo Exhibits
Baseball
Black History
Bob Graham
Bush Years
Daguerreotype to Digital
Everglades
Folklife Postcards
Golf
Harper Collection
Hurricanes
Key West
Jacksonville Fire
Movies
Seminoles

These photographs from the Florida Photographic Collection document the nature, culture, development and conservation of the Florida Everglades, a massive wetland ecosystem that has been the focus of much human activity and as well as debate throughout the 20th Century.

Nature | Culture | Development | Conservation

Seminoles hunting alligators

The first documented peoples in the Everglades were the Calusa and r cultures.

Decimated by disease, they were the Florida Seminoles, who settled Florida during the Second and Third Se

The beauty, ecology, conservation, culture, and development captured in these photographs of the Florida Everglades paint a portrait of **The Everglades in the Time of Marjory Stoneman Douglas.**

water from the Everglades. The water returns to the land as rainfall. Without it, the wetlands would dry up.

In her last chapter entitled "The Eleventh Hour," Douglas wrote: "Yet the springs of fine water had flowed again. The balance still existed between the forces of life and of death. There is a balance in man also. . . . Perhaps even in this last hour, in a new relation of usefulness and beauty, the vast, magnificent, subtle and unique region of the Everglades may not be utterly lost."[8]

This classic work has inspired Americans past and present. It has since been translated into many languages for people to enjoy around the world. President Harry S Truman made the Everglades into a national park the same year the book was published. In his dedication speech, President Truman called the park a "conservation victory."

Soon after the Everglades became a national park, America began the largest water project ever tried anywhere on Earth. The United States has paid millions of dollars and many resources to restore the Everglades wetlands. There is still a great deal of work to do.

In the twenty-first century, people are finding new ways to protect the Everglades. Florida residents are also doing more to protect the wetlands. Staff at Florida's schools and libraries teach people ways to save the Everglades and the plants and animals living there. State and federal governments are funding research. American Indians are sharing their knowledge to help save the wetlands.

AMERICAN INDIANS, SLAVES, AND IMMIGRANTS

The wild and sometimes dangerous environment of the Everglades became a hiding place for American Indians and African slaves in the mid-1800s. Members of the Seminole Indian tribe hid from

U.S. soldiers here to avoid walking the famous "Trail of Tears" to Oklahoma. American Indians in the eastern United States were forced to move when Congress passed the Indian Removal Act of 1830. While some members of the Seminole tribe moved, others bravely hid in the dense brush of Florida's wetlands.

The Seminoles who hid in the Everglades were relatives of the Creek and other native tribes of Florida. They were joined by African slaves who fled the South before and during the Civil War.

▼ *Florida residents, state and federal governments, and American Indians are all working to help save the wetlands.*

The Seminoles and African Americans learned to live in the Everglades to hide from U.S. soldiers.[9]

They had to deal with bad weather and attacks from flesh-eating, blood-sucking insects like flies and mosquitoes. They faced danger from crocodiles, alligators, bears, panthers, wild boars, and poisonous snakes. They hid from the soldiers in this wilderness for many years. Finally, the soldiers gave up; they never did find the Seminoles who had hidden in the Everglades.

In modern times, the Seminoles and other American Indian tribes are important to the Everglades' future. Now American Indians and the U.S. government are working to restore the river of grass. They also help the many plant and animals

APPROVED WEB SITE

Rebellion: John Horse and the Black Seminoles, the First Black Rebels to Beat American Slavery

The Black Seminole warrior John Horse was one of the most successful freedom fighters in U.S. history. This site provides information about the largest slave rebellion in the country's history. It includes interactive maps, images, time lines and essays.

Access this Web site from http://www.myreportlinks.com

of the Everglades by working with scientists. The living creatures of these wetlands have helped American Indians survive for thousands of years.

Their work becomes even more important as the state of Florida grows. Many people are moving to "the Sunshine State" for warmer temperatures. Millions of tourists visit south Florida each year to enjoy its ocean beaches and theme parks, golf courses, and resorts. Florida lawmakers are seeking better ways of managing the needs of people who live in nearby cities to protect life in the Everglades. Many people who work in Florida have jobs in "service" trades, which are often based in cities.[10]

Immigrants are also moving to south Florida from nearby Central and South America, as well as from islands in the Caribbean Sea. They are coming to find jobs, educate their children, and improve their lives. Many of them work in the resort industry, or harvest farm crops. Many Spanish-speaking students are enrolled in Miami and Dade County public schools.

For all of these reasons, it will take people working together to save the Everglades. Their work will help people, plants, and animals in the future to call the "river of grass" their home.

Chapter

2

Water lilies and saw grass under a bright Florida sky.

Never Surrendered

No one knows for sure how the Everglades got its name. The old English word glade means "shiny or bright." It has almost the same meaning in other European languages; it means "place of light." Over time, the word came to mean an open, grassy place under a bright sky.[1]

"Glades" is still the word many people use for the Everglades. It is the perfect word for this place. Picture clouds sailing over smooth water that acts as a mirror. The reflection is broken only by saw grass stalks and floating flowers. People have stood in the hot sun to watch scenes like this in the Everglades for thousands of years.

Early Spanish explorers named the Everglades "Lagoon of the High Spirit" because of its open space, bright light, and wide, blue sky.[2] In the early 1500s, Juan Ponce de León sailed to the North American continent from Spain in search of gold. He claimed to have found a magical spring in Florida that made anyone who bathed in it young again. His quest for "the Fountain of Youth" drew attention in Europe. This story is now an American legend.

A statue of Juan Ponce De León, the Spanish explorer, in St. Augustine, Florida.

JUAN PONCE DE LEON

HE ARRIVED ON EASTER SUNDAY
IN 1513 LOOKING FOR THE
FOUNTAIN OF YOUTH. HE
FOUND SOMETHING BETTER,
A BEAUTIFUL LAND THAT HE
CLAIMED FOR SPAIN, AND HE
CALLED IT FLORIDA.

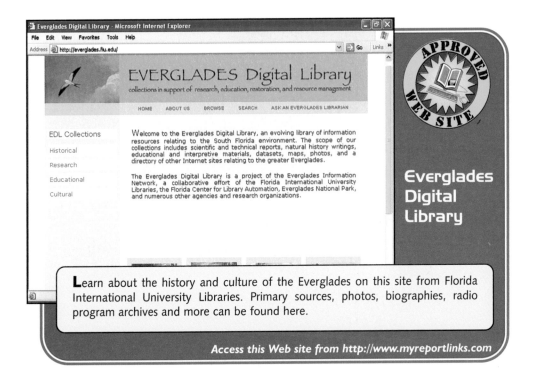

Learn about the history and culture of the Everglades on this site from Florida International University Libraries. Primary sources, photos, biographies, radio program archives and more can be found here.

Access this Web site from http://www.myreportlinks.com

Today, tourists are drawn to St. Augustine, Florida, and the Fountain of Youth Archaeological Park. Here, visitors can drink from the spring that led to the tale of the magic fountain. Unfortunately, today the water has a bitter taste.[3] America's oldest city is located northeast of Everglades National Park.

Europeans returned home and told stories of a strange new land and red-skinned people across the Atlantic. These stories about the "New World" spread. Fortune-seekers began to wonder whether there was hidden treasure on the other side of the vast sea.

Although early European explorers mapped the borders of the Everglades, they could not venture into its wild interior. It is likely that Ponce De León first saw the Timucuans, Florida's early native people, when he arrived on Florida's northeastern shore.[4] In the years that followed, the Spanish explored the area and set up religious missions in Florida. The English and other Europeans fought with the Spanish for control of Florida.

Many American Indians were killed or captured as slaves in these battles. Many of Florida's native peoples died from diseases like smallpox

▲ This photo of saw grass in the Everglades shows why the area became known as "the River of Grass."

that were carried over by explorers from Europe. Their bodies could not fight off the "new" illnesses. Once European explorers arrived, life would never be the same for the native people who lived there. Their long battle to hold on to the land and their traditions had begun.

A CENTRAL SYSTEM

Florida's coasts have beaches covered with crushed seashells. Pelicans flap slowly over the land's edge. Crabs scurry underfoot just a few feet away from stingrays, which glide in with the tide. Beaches and mangrove forests border the Everglades on three sides. This is what explorers saw when they first landed here.

Today the borders of Everglades National Park extend across the southern tip of Florida and the waters to its south. The northern border of the park begins below the middle of the state. It stretches down to the south coast and into the Florida Bay. The "river of grass" does not have a clear beginning or ending point. When freshwater meets saltwater, the result is a mix of water many people call "brackish." The Everglades wetlands form this type of water area, which is known as an estuary.

Manatees are the largest animals that swim in this brackish water. They are plant-eaters that graze on sea grass. Although they are gentle, manatees

Water's Journey: Everglades is a Web documentary based on a two-part PBS film. A series of animations, a historical time line, and educational resources all help to explain the inner workings of the park.

EDITOR'S CHOICE

are too big to have predators. The main threat to the manatees' habitat is collisions with powerboats (more about this may be found in chapter 5).

➡ ONLY LIMESTONE BELOW

Beneath the Everglades is limestone bedrock that shows its history in layers. When Pangaea split the planet's landmass, the part that was to become North America took the Florida peninsula with it. The oldest layer of bedrock formed about 500 million years ago. Fossils show that many prehistoric plants and animals lived in Florida about 200–65 million years ago during the Jurassic and Cretaceous periods, when the sea level was lower and the land was much drier. The peninsula was about three times the size it is today during this time period.[5]

At different times in Earth's history, climate change caused sea levels to rise and fall. The land that is now the Everglades was covered by the ocean after the last Ice Age about ten thousand years ago. Over time, the waters drew back and the land rose up. A plate of mud tilted in a pan of saltwater would make a good model for the Everglades land as it is today. Florida's land juts out like a shelf. It sticks out into the ocean.

FRESHWATER SPRINGS AND CAVES

In some places, the bedrock beneath the Everglades is full of cracks and holes. Underground water flows up through these holes in the rock. In some spots, this flow of filtered water creates freshwater springs, sinkholes, or lakes. Northern and central Florida are home to this type of land, called a Karst terrain.[6]

Some of these natural springs have underwater limestone caves. Many people enjoy diving in these freshwater caves. They swim with sunfish, eels, and manatees in clear, cool waters. Native Floridians know it is always good to keep watch for alligators, even though they do not gather near the caves very often.

Alligators like the dark, murky waters of the Everglades. There are many alligators in Lake Okeechobee, which is located to the north of the

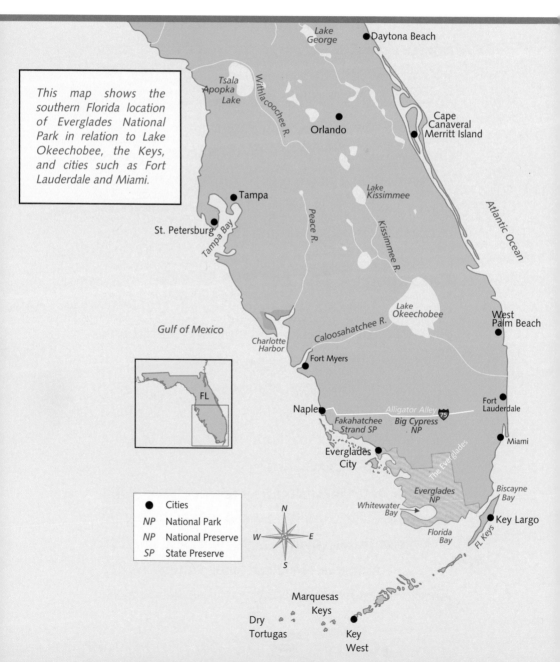

This map shows the southern Florida location of Everglades National Park in relation to Lake Okeechobee, the Keys, and cities such as Fort Lauderdale and Miami.

Lake George

Daytona Beach

Tsala Apopka Lake

Withlacoochee R.

Cape Canaveral
Merritt Island

Orlando

Tampa

Lake Kissimmee

Atlantic Ocean

St. Petersburg
Tampa Bay

Peace R.

Kissimmee R.

Gulf of Mexico

Lake Okeechobee

West Palm Beach

Charlotte Harbor

Caloosahatchee R.

FL

Fort Myers

Fort Lauderdale

Naples

Alligator Alley

75

Fakahatchee Strand SP

Big Cypress NP

Miami

Everglades City

The Everglades

Everglades NP

Biscayne Bay

Cities

NP National Park

NP National Preserve

SP State Preserve

N

W   E

S

Whitewater Bay

Florida Bay

Key Largo

FL Keys

Marquesas Keys

Dry Tortugas

Key West

Everglades. Here the ground is so full of water, it can hold no more. Rainwater collects in Lake Okeechobee. This is the source of the Everglades.

Several smaller rivers and waterways flow in all directions from Lake Okeechobee. American Indians call it "Big Water." Cattle ranches, sugarcane farms, and American Indian reservations now border Lake Okeechobee, which is the second-largest freshwater lake wholly within the confines of the United States.

In the southern part of Everglades National Park, a maze of mangrove trees separates the saw grass river from ocean tides. Still farther south, neon-colored coral sways in the waves of a warm sea. Beyond the coral reef, dolphins leap, schools of barracuda dart, and sharks cruise the ocean. Beyond this lies a chain of islands known as the Florida Keys. Less than 100 miles (160.9 kilometers) across the Atlantic Ocean from "the Keys" is the nation of Cuba. Beyond Cuba lies a chain of islands in the Caribbean Sea stretching into the open Atlantic.

FLORIDA'S FIRST PEOPLE

When early explorers came upon the Everglades five hundred years ago, they found an uncharted wilderness full of secrets. This means it was not fully drawn on maps. The Everglades has inspired tales of supernatural powers in people and animals.

For example, one story that has been passed on from the Seminole tribe is about an animal changing the weather. As the story goes, a rabbit awoke a sleeping frog. To make the rabbit go away, the frog croaked to call the rain. Not wanting to get wet, the rabbit took off.[7]

The Timucuans were among Florida's first people. This tribe lived along the St. John's River and the northeastern coast. There they found plenty of animals and freshwater fish for food, as well as fruit-bearing plants and trees for wood. They hunted with spears, and later, bows and arrows.

Farther south, the Caloosa people made their living from the ocean. The Caloosa (or "Calusa," as it is sometimes spelled) did not have to go too far into the wetlands for what they needed. They traveled along the coastal islands in dugout canoes. For food, they could gather shellfish or catch fish farther out to sea.

NAMES OF AMERICAN INDIAN HERITAGE

The Caloosahatchee River carries on the name of these early coastal dwellers. This river stretches to the west from Lake Okeechobee to the Gulf of Mexico. Major cities, such as Tampa and Miami, were also named by Florida's American Indians. For example, the Miccosukee and Seminole tribes named Miami. Many towns, schools, rivers, lakes,

This photograph from 1926 shows a group of Seminole Indians, whose forefathers inhabited the Everglades.

and parks across the state are named with words from one of Florida's native languages.

The Tequesta and Apalachee were also among Florida's first peoples. Like the Timucuans and the Caloosa, they used poles and palmetto branches to build homes with floors above the ground. This helped keep insects, snakes, and other creatures out. These tribes farmed crops and harvested fruit and vegetables for food.

Over time, early natives married people from other clans or from tribes that came from the north. Many spoke Hitchiti, an early native language. In the 1700s, native people from the Muskogee and Creek tribes from Georgia and Alabama moved southward away from European colonies.[8] They joined with other native people in Florida to form what we now know as the Seminole and Miccosukee tribes. They call themselves the "unconquered" or "free people."

THREE SEMINOLE WARS

In 1816, American soldiers led by General Andrew Jackson marched into Florida to fight both the Spanish, who controlled the land, and the American Indians who lived there. This began the start of the three famous "Seminole Wars." Spain agreed to sell Florida to the U.S. government five years later. Jackson began his term as U.S. president in 1829.

The U.S. Congress passed the Indian Removal Act of 1830 one year later. This caused some of the Seminoles to flee far into the swamplands. They would not walk the famous "Trail of Tears" to new land in Oklahoma along with their relatives and other native tribes.

Three Seminole leaders named Micanopy, Jumper, and Alligator led hundreds of native warriors to attack U.S. soldiers. They killed most of the soldiers. This started the Second Seminole War in 1835.

Seminole Chief Osceola led many brave battles against U.S. soldiers. He led the Seminole warriors to ambush U.S. soldiers—and then quickly retreated

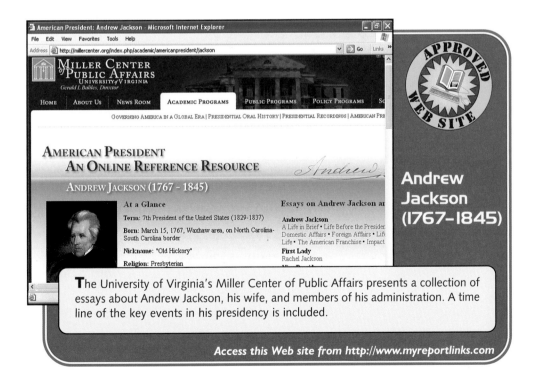

The University of Virginia's Miller Center of Public Affairs presents a collection of essays about Andrew Jackson, his wife, and members of his administration. A time line of the key events in his presidency is included.

Access this Web site from http://www.myreportlinks.com

deep into the Everglades swamps. This plan worked well for the Seminoles, who knew how to survive the dangers of the Everglades. It gave them an edge in their fight with the soldiers, who did not know much about the river of grass. The Seminoles could easily launch surprise attacks, then quickly retreat into the dense brush to avoid capture. General Zachary Taylor led U.S. troops during this time. Like Jackson, he would later be elected president.

A year after the battle that started the second war, Chief Osceola became ill. He agreed to meet with the U.S. government to work out a peaceful treaty soon after. But soldiers captured Osceola when he arrived at the meeting. They put him in

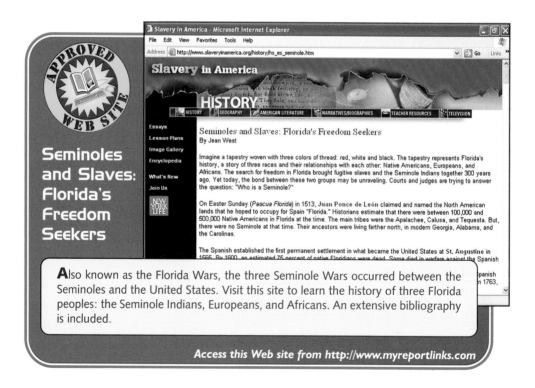

Seminoles and Slaves: Florida's Freedom Seekers

Also known as the Florida Wars, the three Seminole Wars occurred between the Seminoles and the United States. Visit this site to learn the history of three Florida peoples: the Seminole Indians, Europeans, and Africans. An extensive bibliography is included.

Access this Web site from http://www.myreportlinks.com

prison, where he died. This further angered many Seminole people and made them even more determined to fight for their homeland.

African-American slaves sometimes fled slave owners in the South and joined with the Seminoles. U.S. soldiers found runaway slaves as they searched for hidden Seminole camps. This second war lasted seven years and cost the United States millions of dollars to fight. By the end of this war, hundreds of Seminoles had survived by hiding out in Big Cypress Swamp and other parts of the Everglades.

Soon after Florida became a U.S. state in 1845, the U.S. government again tried to urge the last Seminole holdouts to leave. They invited Seminole Chief Billy Bowlegs to Washington, D.C., in hopes of talking him into moving the tribe to Oklahoma. Still the Seminole chief would not move. This led to the Third Seminole War in 1855.

U.S. soldiers burned Bowlegs's camp and destroyed the tribe's food supply. They finally captured Bowlegs in 1858. About half of the Seminoles moved west to Indian Territory in Oklahoma; the rest stayed in the Everglades. This ended the Seminole Wars.

THE SEMINOLES WHO STAYED

After the third war, many Seminoles stayed in the Everglades and lived much like their parents and grandparents who had hid from soldiers in the wetlands. They raised cattle, chicken, and pigs deep in the swamp. They planted crops such as corn and pumpkins, and built special huts that were well hidden within the brush. They never left the Everglades.

When the U.S. Congress passed the Indian Reorganization Act in 1934, it allowed American Indians to govern themselves under their own laws on reservation lands. A few years later, the U.S. government set aside about 80,000 acres (32,400 hectares) in Florida for the Seminoles.

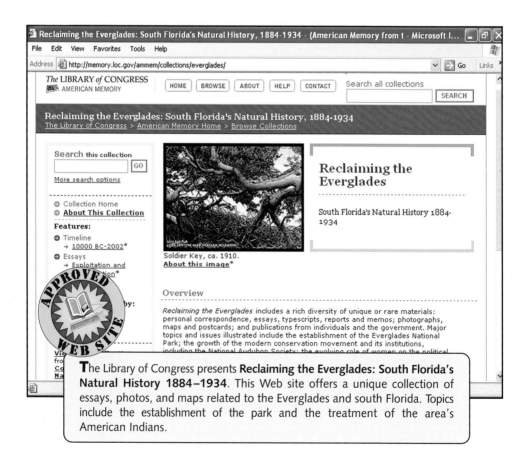

The Library of Congress presents **Reclaiming the Everglades: South Florida's Natural History 1884–1934**. This Web site offers a unique collection of essays, photos, and maps related to the Everglades and south Florida. Topics include the establishment of the park and the treatment of the area's American Indians.

They were officially recognized as a nation by the United States two decades later.

Today, about a thousand Seminoles and Miccosukees own nearly 100,000 acres (40,470 hectares) of reservation land throughout Florida. Their land is separated into different areas. Seminole tribal headquarters is located in Hollywood, near Fort Lauderdale. The Miccosukee branch of the Seminole tribe lives in the Everglades. There are also Seminole reservations in Brighton, Fort Pierce, Immokalee, Tampa, and Hollywood, Florida.

Modern Seminoles make their living through farming and businesses, including Everglades tourism. Visitors enjoy attending Seminole rodeos. These shows are special in that they often have alligator wrestling. Today's Seminoles own cattle ranches, harvest crops, and run a casino.

Yet they have also managed to hold on to their traditions and culture. Tribal members still have names like Jumper, Micco, and Osceola. They carry on the names of their brave leaders who would not give up the Everglades.

⇨ UNCONQUERED CULTURE

In early summer, many branches of Seminoles come together to celebrate the Green Corn Ceremony, the tribe's most important holiday. While the Seminoles perform other ceremonies in the company of outsiders, they hold their annual

Green Corn Dance in a secret location. It is closed to anyone who is not a member of the tribe, and the celebration lasts several days.

During the ceremony, the tribe's leader starts a special fire. He keeps the fire burning through the night as he leads prayers on behalf of the tribe. The Seminoles believe that skipping the corn ceremony could result in hard times for the tribe in the coming year.

During celebration days, tribal members perform the Stomp Dance in beautiful patchwork clothing. They have mastered the craft of creating smooth, light clothes decorated with patterns in bold colors. They display long racks of these garments for tourists in roadside shops, at rodeos, and at other events in the Everglades.

⊖KEEPING TRADITIONS ALIVE

The Seminoles feast on traditional food such as sofkee, which is a type of corn gruel. In the past, Seminole families kept a pot of sofkee simmering on a cooking fire throughout the day. A person simply ate whenever he or she was hungry. Seminoles also enjoy a strong, black drink called Asi, which is made from dried leaves. Pumpkin fry bread, deer sausages, citrus smoothies, and Indian Taco Salad are also Seminole favorites.

Seminoles and other Florida cooks serve chunks of roasted alligator, which they also sell to tourists. Alligator meat is served with barbecue sauce as "fast food" throughout the Everglades. The meat is similar to lean pork. Folks also enjoy turtle soup and frog legs.

While many Seminoles live in modern houses with air-conditioning, their community centers are still made from huts called chickees. These dwellings have no walls. Usually, a chickee hut is made of a cypress wood frame with a thatched roof made of palm fronds.

The hut is the perfect building for this type of climate. The palm frond roof provides cool shade, yet the hut remains open to allow breezes to pass through. The Seminoles learned to build these huts as a way of surviving Florida's hot, humid weather.

Chapter 3

Marjory Stoneman Douglas, author of *The Everglades: River of Grass*, worked tirelessly to protect the Everglades. This photo was taken at her home in the 1920s.

Guardians of the Saw Grass

The warm, wet landscape of south Florida has drawn farmers for well over a century. Citrus fruits like orange and grapefruit need plenty of sunshine and rain. The Everglades has both.

Tobacco and sugar plantations spread across America's South in the late 1800s. During this time, some farmers headed to the Florida peninsula from states like Virginia, the Carolinas, Georgia, and Alabama. They began draining water from the Everglades for sugar, citrus, and other crops. This marked the beginning of a time of great change in the Everglades.

In the decades that followed, the U.S. government helped farmers by building a system that changed the flow of water throughout the wetlands. They did not think their actions would cause harm. They believed draining land to grow more crops was good because it helped provide food for America.

Back then, many people saw the Everglades as a worthless "swamp." At the time, few understood that the survival of Everglades land—and all life upon it—relied on the natural direction of the water's flow. Rainwater flowing southward is what keeps this ecosystem balanced. For thousands of years, rainwater has collected in the center of the state, then washed down over 10,000 square miles (25,900 square kilometers) of mostly saw grass through mangrove forests, over beaches, and into the ocean.

Florida's weather during the early 1900s was harsh. A series of hurricanes destroyed homes, farms, and business projects and killed many people. The Mediterranean Citrus fruit fly ruined crops.

The Tamiami Trail, a highway that connects the cities of Tampa and Miami, opened in 1928. The Florida Park Service was created in 1935. Cypress Gardens, a popular spot for Florida tourists, opened in 1936 in Winter Haven.

FLAGLER'S FOLLY

Flooding during the yearly wet season is an important part of the Glades' natural cycle. But people who settled Florida wanted to control floods on farms, or near their homes in the state's fast-growing cities. In the early 1900s, railroads were built to carry people south to new towns such as Fort Lauderdale on the state's eastern coast and Miami to its south. Roads were built to Fort Myers on the Gulf of Mexico and Tampa to its north. Then even more of the Everglades was drained to make room for highways, hospitals, and schools.

One of the men who built Florida's railroads was Henry Flagler, who founded the Standard Oil Company with John D. Rockefeller in New York. After the death of his wife, Mary, in 1881, Flagler began to spend more time in Florida with his young son.[1]

Flagler wanted to build hotels and a railroad to bring tourists to Florida. He built the Florida East Coast Railway, which stretched from St. Augustine

Henry Morrison Flagler Museum

Whitehall is the fifty-five-room mansion in Palm Beach, Florida, that Henry Flagler built for his wife. It's now the site of the Henry Morrison Flagler Museum. The museum's Web site includes a biography of Flagler and details about the building of Florida's East Coast Railway.

Access this Web site from http://www.myreportlinks.com

in the northern part of the peninsula to Key West, the most southern point in America.

In 1905, he began building a railroad that would span 7 miles (11.2 kilometers) of open ocean. This railroad later became known as "Flagler's Folly." Workers on the project had to deal with biting sand flies and mosquitoes, as well as bad storms and hurricanes. Hundreds died in a hurricane in 1906. Despite these troubles, trains on the railroad made their first runs in 1912. But it did not draw enough passengers to make money. Flagler's Folly was finally destroyed by a hurricane on Labor Day in 1935.

Still, sunny skies, warm weather, and wild beauty made south Florida a popular vacation spot. By the mid-1900s, more families owned cars. Shops and shows sprang up to entertain Everglades tourists along the roads. Hotels, restaurants, swimming pools, sports fields, golf courses—all of these things took land and water from the river of saw grass.

"ONE OF A KIND" PLACE

President Harry S Truman gave a speech during the ceremony held on December 6, 1947, to celebrate the opening of Everglades National Park. He was excited about the idea of setting aside nearly 500,000 acres (202,350 hectares) of land to protect plants and animals of the Everglades. Just a year before, President Truman had begun visiting Key West to get away from the stress of working in

▲ *President Harry S Truman speaking at the opening ceremony of Everglades National Park.*

Washington, D.C., the nation's capital. The house he stayed in became known as the "Little White House," and other U.S. presidents have used it after him.

At Everglades National Park's opening ceremony, Truman said, "Here are no lofty peaks seeking the sky, no mighty glaciers or rushing streams wearing away the uplifted land. Here is land tranquil in its quiet beauty . . . spectacular plant and animal life that distinguishes this place from all others in our country."[2] He spoke these words twenty years after the first acres of Everglades land on Paradise Key were set aside as

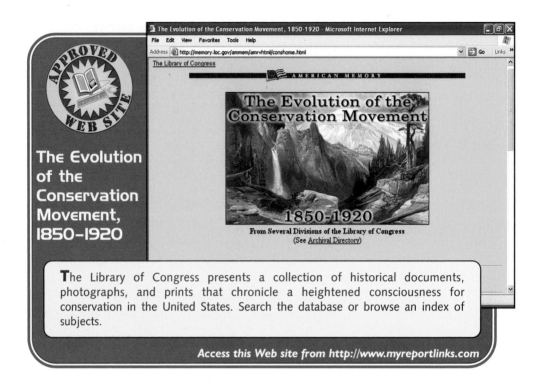

The Evolution of the Conservation Movement, 1850-1920

The Evolution
of the
Conservation
Movement,
1850-1920

The Library of Congress presents a collection of historical documents, photographs, and prints that chronicle a heightened consciousness for conservation in the United States. Search the database or browse an index of subjects.

Access this Web site from http://www.myreportlinks.com

Royal Palm State Park. This land later became part of the larger park. A small group of people had worked to have the land set aside for Everglades's plants and animals. It was a place where they could live as they had for centuries in the wild.

Most Americans in the first half of the twentieth century viewed south Florida as open space where new homes and businesses could be built. Only a few recognized that the river of grass was a wilderness in need of protection. One of these people was the first director of the National Park Service, Stephen T. Mather. He presented his idea of making the Everglades a national park to the U.S. secretary of the interior in 1923.[3]

A few years later, a landscape architect from the Northeast named Ernest F. Coe moved to Miami's Coconut Grove neighborhood. Coe found himself drawn to the river of saw grass and vowed to protect it. He formed a group of government and business leaders to create Everglades National Park.

"Father of the Everglades"

Coe wrote a letter to Mather to ask his help in creating a national park in the lower Everglades wetlands.[4] They worked together to gain the help of U.S. senators and representatives in Congress. In 1930, a group of experts began drawing up plans that would create borders for the park. The group included Marjory Stoneman Douglas, author of the famous book *The Everglades: River of Grass,* mentioned in chapter 1.

President Franklin D. Roosevelt signed the bill to set aside Everglades land as a national park in 1934. It took another thirteen years to open the park. Coe earned the nickname "Father of the Everglades" for his hard work. In 1996, four decades after Coe's death, the park opened a new visitor center bearing his name.

Even though more citizens had begun to value the wildlife of the Everglades, large numbers of people were moving to south Florida. This put more demands on the land and water of the Everglades. In 1948, the U.S. Army Corps of Engineers started the Central and South Florida Project to build roads, canals, and levees to direct the flow of water to farmers and residents, as well as to the national park. Their goal was to stop seasonal flooding in some areas. The engineers worked with a state agency called the South Florida Water Management District, which has led the control of water flows in the Everglades ever since.

In the late 1900s, the U.S. government expanded parklands. Then a number of laws were passed in

▽ Ernest F. Coe became known as the "Father of the Everglades" for his efforts in bringing about the formation of the park. This visitor center named after Coe opened in 1996.

Florida by the state and federal government in the 1980s to 1990s to control the use of land and limit the growth of cities near the Everglades. Some of these laws were passed after long court battles with farmers about phosphorous, a chemical that pollutes the wetlands in the form of toxic runoff. Courts have ordered farmers to change their practices and help restore parts of the wetlands.

⊜ FRIENDS OF THE EVERGLADES

If Coe is Everglades National Park's "father," then few would argue that Marjory Stoneman Douglas could be called its modern-day "mother." Marjory Stoneman Douglas worked as a reporter for her father at the *Miami Herald* newspaper. She became a well-known writer who also grew famous for her direct way of speaking, and devoted her life to taking care of the Everglades. In 1970, she formed Friends of the Everglades. This group still works to protect the Everglades today.

Marjory Stoneman Douglas often wore a big, floppy hat and large glasses, even when she spoke in public. In a 1987 book about her life, *Voice of the River,* a man jokes that she had a way of speaking that silenced everyone—even mosquitoes![5] She called upon the U.S. Army Corps of Engineers to be good stewards, or caretakers, of the wetlands. She also won court battles on behalf of the Everglades. Some of these cases were about whether farmers or business owners could build near park lands. Others were about how waste from cities or fertilizers from farms flows into the Glades' wetlands. Others were about ways to help endangered animal species.

Majory Stoneman Douglas died in 1998 at the age of 108. True to her wishes, her ashes were spread in the river of grass. Through the words of her famous book, her voice is still "heard" by many people today. As she wrote, "There are no other Everglades in the world. Nothing anywhere else is like them; their vast glittering openness, wider than the enormous visible round of the horizon. . . ."[6]

In 2007, the Everglades ecosystem is less than half of its original size. Many plant and animal

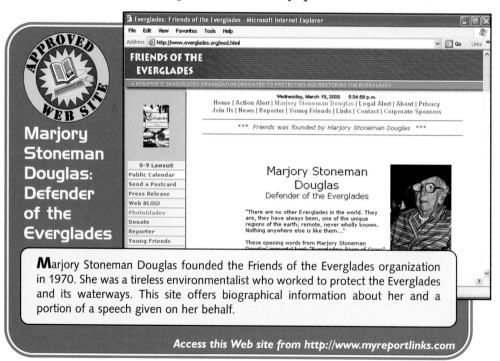

Marjory Stoneman Douglas: Defender of the Everglades

Marjory Stoneman Douglas founded the Friends of the Everglades organization in 1970. She was a tireless environmentalist who worked to protect the Everglades and its waterways. This site offers biographical information about her and a portion of a speech given on her behalf.

Access this Web site from http://www.myreportlinks.com

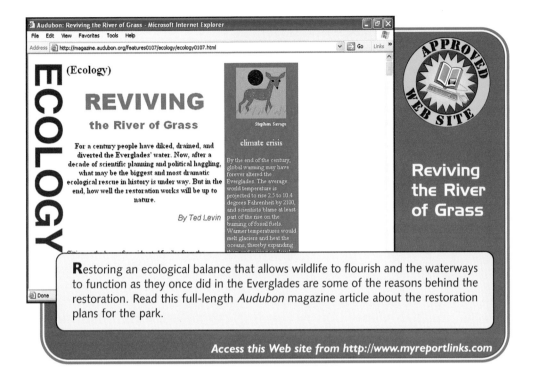

ECOLOGY

(Ecology)

REVIVING
the River of Grass

For a century people have diked, drained, and diverted the Everglades' water. Now, after a decade of scientific planning and political haggling, what may be the biggest and most dramatic ecological rescue in history is under way. But in the end, how well the restoration works will be up to nature.

By Ted Levin

Stephen Savage

climate crisis

By the end of the century, global warming may have forever altered the Everglades. The average world temperature is projected to rise 2.5 to 10.4 degrees Fahrenheit by 2100, and scientists blame at least part of the rise on the burning of fossil fuels. Warmer temperatures would melt glaciers and heat the oceans, thereby expanding

Reviving the River of Grass

Restoring an ecological balance that allows wildlife to flourish and the waterways to function as they once did in the Everglades are some of the reasons behind the restoration. Read this full-length *Audubon* magazine article about the restoration plans for the park.

Access this Web site from http://www.myreportlinks.com

species are in danger of becoming extinct. But there has been one critical change that could mean a better future for the Everglades. Thanks to the hard work of people in the last century, the Everglades is now seen as a special place. Many people favor protecting what is left of the Everglades beyond the year 2000. The National Park Service, farmers, and American Indians all play important roles in protecting this watery wilderness. People across the globe now see the Everglades as worth saving.

Chapter 4

A great egret, one of the many wading birds in the Everglades, photographed among cypress trees.

Mangroves and Mermaids

The Everglades is known around the world for its tall, colorful wading birds. Bird-watchers flock to Everglades National Park to gaze at life in the sky and along south Florida's shorelines.

Wading birds against the wild backdrop of these wetlands are also favorite subjects for artists and photographers. The birds stand in the shallow water to pluck fish, snails, and insects for their meals. From a walkway, car, or boat, they look like they are from the age of dinosaurs. In the past, these birds were hunted for their feathers, which were used to decorate ladies' hats. Overhunting soon became a problem in the second half of the nineteenth century. Hunting is illegal today.

→ BIRDS OF A BIGGER FEATHER

One bird many see in the Everglades is the great egret, which stands over 3 feet (0.91 meters) tall. It is a foot taller than its cousin,

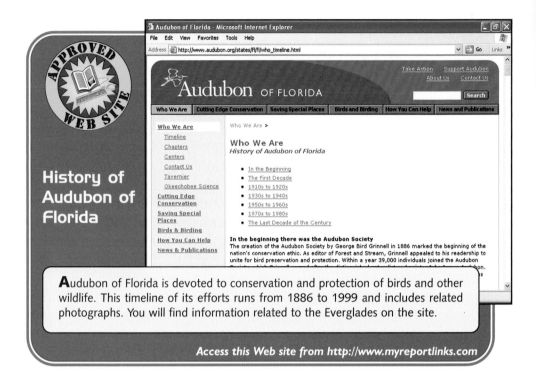

Audubon of Florida is devoted to conservation and protection of birds and other wildlife. This timeline of its efforts runs from 1886 to 1999 and includes related photographs. You will find information related to the Everglades on the site.

Access this Web site from http://www.myreportlinks.com

the snowy egret. A larger bird is the wood stork, which has a featherless, black head. The slender, white ibis is a bit smaller.

Another wading bird that makes the Everglades its home is the limpkin. It walks with an odd gait, like a limp; this is how it got its name.[1] It has drab, brown feathers with white marks. It stands about two feet (half a meter) tall and has a long, curved beak for pulling snails from the water. People who live in the Glades know its low, wailing call.

People in the Everglades often see the great blue heron, which stands over 4 feet (1.2 meters) tall. Its smaller cousin, the tricolored heron, is half its size.

Zipping around the legs of these wading birds are ducks, coots, and grebes. They quietly bob among lily pads. The Everglades is home to a thousand plants that provide food and shelter for birds.

The Florida sandhill crane is sometimes mistaken for the great blue heron. It is nearly 4 feet (1.2 meters) tall and lives mostly in prairie marshes along the Kissimmee River. Although it lives in south Florida year-round, it is joined in winter months by its cousin, the greater sandhill crane. These large birds fly in from as far away as Siberia and are easy to spot. When they call out, they make a sound like a bugle.[2]

EFFORTS TO SAVE THE BIRDS

Conservation groups are working to save birds in the Everglades. In recent years, scientists have banded roseate spoonbills, which are wading birds named for the shape of their beaks. Inside their bills are little "fingers" that help them catch small fish, insects, and mollusks in the mud. They have smooth feathers that are pretty shades of pink. Many were overhunted for their feathers. They live along the Gulf Coast, in mangrove swamps, and at Ten Thousand Islands to the south.

The double-crested cormorant and anhinga dive in the water for their food. Their black feathers look shiny and wet nearly all of the time. Both are just under 3 feet (0.91 meters) tall. The anhinga has a strange way of drying off its feathers. It stands with its wings spread out to catch the sunshine and breeze. One could say it drip dries.

⊜COLD-BLOODED REPTILES

In the shadow of the anhinga's black wings are reptiles. All are cold-blooded, which means they keep their body temperature up by staying in warm places or in the sun. To stay cool, they burrow

▽ *Roseate spoonbills are pink-feathered wading birds named for the shape of their beaks. Their beaks contain tiny "fingers" that help them catch small fish and other prey.*

▲ *Alligators sometimes pile on top of one another in a giant heap while enjoying the sun.*

underground. Some, like the American alligator or the American crocodile, are quite large. Although the alligator is usually larger, both can grow to more than 10 feet (3.1 meters) long.

On cooler mornings, alligators climb onto land to find a spot in the sun. When they run out of room, they pile on top of one another to form one giant, scaly pyramid. Sometimes alligators will pile up in the middle of a road. If a car or even a

The Nature Conservancy, a nonprofit organization with chapters in every state and more than thirty countries, has managed to protect more than one hundred million acres of land and thousands of miles of rivers. Take an online tour at its Web site.

EDITOR'S CHOICE

school bus approaches, they may not move. This means the stalled vehicle might have to wait to move until the alligators wake up!

There are subtle differences between an alligator and a crocodile. The crocodile has a long snout and every fourth tooth sticks out when it closes its mouth. The alligator's snout is broad. Alligators live all over Florida, while crocodiles live only in the brackish, salty water off the coast and around the mangrove swamps.

Unlike crocodiles, gators can walk some distance on land. But alligators tend to run in a straight line once they are out of the water. If an alligator chases someone on land, one possible way to escape is to run in a slanted direction (like a football player). This makes it harder for the alligator to track movements. Of course, it's best to avoid being chased by an alligator at all! Florida residents know to avoid wading in shallow ponds and the murky waters of the Everglades.

Many people who live in the area have learned to recognize the grunting sound an alligator makes. But alligators can be difficult to spot. It is important to avoid swimming in ponds or lakes in Florida that might be home to alligators—even if

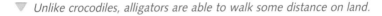 Unlike crocodiles, alligators are able to walk some distance on land.

none are visible. Even though alligator attacks are rare, they are wild reptiles and their behavior is unpredictable.

Mangrove forests are home to crocodiles. Mangrove trees are special because they can take freshwater out of saltwater. Their roots block salt, and they also lose salt through their leaves. The appearance of red mangroves is different from other kinds of trees because their roots jut out of the water. For this reason, some say the root systems of red mangroves make them look like "walking trees."

Black and white mangroves have a different kind of root system. There are nearly 500,000 acres (202,350 hectares) of mangrove forests in

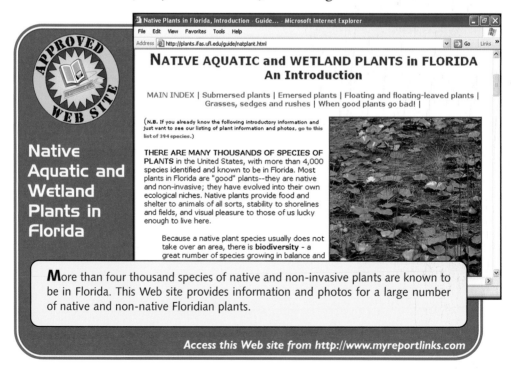

More than four thousand species of native and non-invasive plants are known to be in Florida. This Web site provides information and photos for a large number of native and non-native Floridian plants.

Access this Web site from http://www.myreportlinks.com

south Florida. This maze of trees blocks waves, winds, and floods, and even traps pollution between the ocean and land.

Stretched across mangrove branches and roots are webs made by spiders like the golden orb weaver. It has yellow, white, and black coloring. It cleans its web of leaves and sticks every day so that the insects it preys upon do not see it.[3] Some of the most common insects in the Everglades are horseflies and lubber grasshoppers. Either of these might be caught in the web of this kind of spider.

Some spider webs are even large enough to trap birds and bats. But the main source of food for many insects and spiders, and for many fish, is mosquitoes (see chapter 5). There are more than sixty different kinds of mosquito in the Everglades. They are eaten by small fish, which in turn are eaten by larger fish, which are then consumed by reptiles, birds, and mammals.

➲ Not Fish Food

The main source of food for wading birds and alligators is fish. One of the larger fish is the Florida gar, which measures 3 feet (0.91 meter) long. It has sharp teeth and thick scales. It needs to swim to the water's surface often. But it is rarely eaten. Gar eggs are poisonous to other animals, and so they are not preyed upon. This gives gar offspring

The golden orb weaver's coloring is yellow, black, and white. It keeps its web invisible to prey by cleaning it of sticks and leaves each day.

a better chance of surviving. Small mosquito fish are only two (5.1 centimeters) inches long and are a source of food for birds and larger fish. These insect-eaters are found across the park.

The eastern indigo snake shares the Everglades with all of these other cold-blooded creatures. These snakes are bluish black with red or orange markings on their heads, and will often grow up to eight feet (2.4 meters) in length. They are not poisonous, but they will flatten their necks, hiss, strike, and (very rarely) bite a human if cornered. The males fight and kill the young of other snakes. Females lay their eggs in old burrows made by the gopher tortoise or other animals. Skunks and raccoons raid the

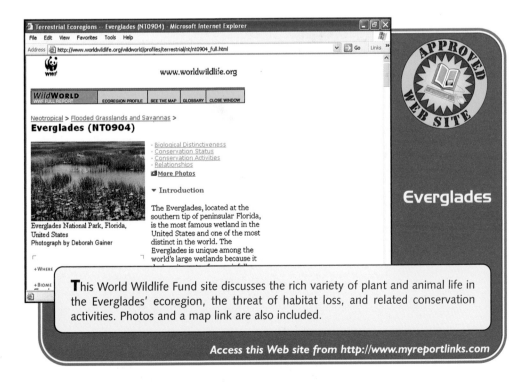

This World Wildlife Fund site discusses the rich variety of plant and animal life in the Everglades' ecoregion, the threat of habitat loss, and related conservation activities. Photos and a map link are also included.

Access this Web site from http://www.myreportlinks.com

burrows and eat the white, tough-shelled eggs.
Young snakes are also in danger of being preyed
upon by hawks or owls.

ON THE PROWL

Hunting in the hammocks of the Big Cypress
National Preserve, as well as Everglades National
Park, is the Florida panther, the state animal. It is
in danger of dying out; its numbers have reached
well below a hundred in recent years.[4] The Florida
panther grows up to seven feet (2.1 meters) long
and will travel up to 20 miles (32.2 kilometers) in
a day to stalk white-tailed deer.

Key deer, also an endangered species and
"cousin" of the white-tailed deer, live on islands
off Florida's southern coast called "the Keys." Key
deer are the smallest American deer. They weigh
less than 100 pounds (45.4 kilograms) when full
grown. There is a U.S. Fish and Wildlife Service
refuge for these deer on Big Pine Key.[5]

Panthers sometimes cross paths with Florida
black bears. These 200-pound (90.7-kilogram)
predators roam the same area as wild boars, bob-
cats, and panthers. Black bears will tear open a
beehive to eat the honey inside. However, all of
these large animals would run from a swarm of
fire ants. These ants are not native to the Everglades. Their bites leave huge welts on skin. They
will take over a victim in a matter of seconds.

Key deer, an endangered species, live in the Florida "Keys," or islands off the state's southern coast. They weigh less than one hundred pounds when full-grown.

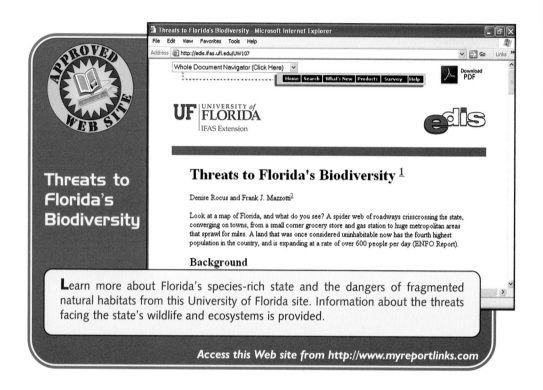

Threats to Florida's Biodiversity

Threats to Florida's Biodiversity - Microsoft Internet Explorer

File   Edit   View   Favorites   Tools   Help

Address http://edis.ifas.ufl.edu/UW107   Go   Links

Whole Document Navigator (Click Here)

Home | Search | What's New | Products | Survey | Help

Download PDF

UF | UNIVERSITY of FLORIDA
IFAS Extension

edis

Threats to Florida's Biodiversity [1]

Denise Rocus and Frank J. Mazzotti[2]

Look at a map of Florida, and what do you see? A spider web of roadways crisscrossing the state, converging on towns, from a small corner grocery store and gas station to huge metropolitan areas that sprawl for miles. A land that was once considered uninhabitable now has the fourth highest population in the country, and is expanding at a rate of over 600 people per day (ENFO Report).

Background

Learn more about Florida's species-rich state and the dangers of fragmented natural habitats from this University of Florida site. Information about the threats facing the state's wildlife and ecosystems is provided.

Access this Web site from http://www.myreportlinks.com

Many people are concerned about the fate of the burrowing owl. This small raptor makes its home in holes, or burrows, on dry land. As more people move to south Florida, cities grow and occupy the land that these owls need for their homes. People are working with the government and wildlife groups to protect them.

The mangrove fox squirrel would give any predator a good chase. It has different colors on its fur than its North American cousins. It is black or brown, with orange sides, belly, rump, and tail. It lives in Florida's rocky pine forests to the north and eats seeds, nuts, and buds.

Bald eagles and osprey are two Everglades birds of prey that eat mostly fish. They can be spotted throughout the park. They build their nests near lagoons and can eat both freshwater and saltwater fish. In recent years, people have worked to provide places for birds of prey to nest in the Everglades. For example, they have built platforms for osprey near water throughout the area. This has given these graceful birds places to build nests.

The Everglade kite is an endangered species. It is also known as the "snail kite" because it mainly eats apple snails. The bird has a hooked beak to help it work snails out of their shells. These raptors are dark colored; males are gray, while females and offspring are brown. Both the male and female have a white patch on the tail.

Everglade kites live in freshwater marshes where the snail is found. These are located in the northern part of the park and around Lake Okee-chobee. Because their range is limited to this small area, they are in danger of becoming extinct. Threats to snails are also threats to the kites.[6] The two species depend on each other for survival.

GENTLE GIANTS

Near the hammocks, raptors glide on hot winds over cabbage palm trees. Among the mangroves, they hunt for fish and insects. In estuaries, they

An Everglade kite—also known as the snail kite—is an endangered raptor species.

may see West Indian manatees rise to the surface for air, which they do about every fifteen minutes.

Manatees are a favorite among tourists. They are so large that they really do "weigh a ton." Yet they float easily throughout the brackish waters surrounding the Everglades.

⇒ MISTAKEN FOR MERMAIDS?

Sometimes manatees swim inland to find sea grass, their main food. Or they venture inland in search of warmer temperatures. Manatees can only live in water that is 68 degrees Fahrenheit (20 degrees Celsius) or warmer. They sometimes gather in ponds surrounding Florida's nuclear power plants, which have warm water. They also live in groups in the waters of the Crystal and St. John's rivers, as well as the Gulf and Atlantic coasts.

In the past, sailors mistook manatees for mermaids. Although manatees do have wide flippers at the base of their tails—like mermaids of legend—most would agree manatees do not look like women!

Also called "sea cows," manatees are plant-eating mammals that are distant cousins of the elephant. Their snouts are much like an elephant's trunk, but shorter. Their front fins have white toenails, and they have wiry hair on their backs (like elephants). But their behavior is gentler than their

An endangered West Indian manatee swims with her calf.

land-roving cousins. They are friendly, curious, and will often approach humans.

It is easy to spot a manatee from a kayak or canoe, but it takes time. Watch for a series of silver dollar-sized bubbles a few minutes before the manatee slowly rises to the surface. Those people who are lucky enough to see a manatee in the wild will make eye contact with a gentle giant.

AN UNDERSEA GARDEN

The coastline around Everglades National Park is surrounded by coral reef gardens. Coral reefs consist of living and also nonliving things. Coral begins as tiny sea animals called coral polyps. These animals release a coating on their own bodies. When they die, they leave this "skeleton" behind and it remains part of the larger reef.

Scuba and snorkel divers enjoy the bold colors of coral reef gardens. But divers must not touch coral—even accidentally. Boat anchors can easily crush part of a reef. It does not take much weight or force to harm coral.

Florida's coral reefs not only look pretty, but they also protect the shoreline from strong ocean waves. Coral provides food and shelter for underwater plants and animals as well. Yet reefs grow very slowly—only about a dozen feet in hundreds, or even thousands, of years![7]

To help save coral, Florida opened the John Pennekamp Coral Reef State Park, the world's first underwater park, in the 1960s. A decade later, the Florida Keys National Marine Sanctuary was opened by the U.S. government. From the air, the reefs make a rainbow-like fortress around the golden sheen of the Everglades.

Chapter

5

Brazilian pepper is considered one of the most invasive plants in Florida. It competes with the native vegetation and has taken over many mangrove forests.

Food Chain Invaders and Other Threats

Mosquitoes provide food for birds and fish. Because of this, they are an important part of the Everglades food chain. Millions of them swarm over mud and saw grass every day.

But they are a problem for people and animals. Even though it is rare, a mosquito can carry a disease and infect a person with its bite. West Nile virus, encephalitis ("en-sef-al-i-tis"), and malaria are diseases that can cause high fever, coma, or even death to their victims.

The threat of disease spread by mosquitoes in the Everglades is serious enough to need the help of government. Experts spray chemicals to kill mosquitoes and prevent disease outbreaks. Emergency response plans are in place should an outbreak occur.

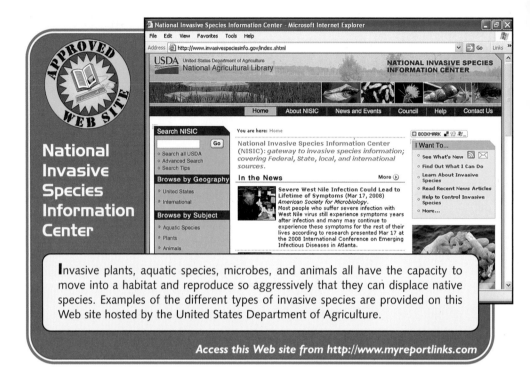

Invasive plants, aquatic species, microbes, and animals all have the capacity to move into a habitat and reproduce so aggressively that they can displace native species. Examples of the different types of invasive species are provided on this Web site hosted by the United States Department of Agriculture.

Access this Web site from http://www.myreportlinks.com

But this approach is unlikely to be a long-term solution to the problem. There is always the chance that chemicals can harm plants and animals, which only serves to keep the Everglades out of balance. Nonchemical ways of controlling mosquitoes can help. For example, one should avoid leaving standing water around because mosquitoes can breed in it. These insects breed easily and are *not* in danger of becoming extinct. A million eggs may hatch within just a few square feet.

Since mosquitoes are more active in the early morning and at dusk, it is a good idea for people to wear long sleeves, pants, and insect repellent during these hours. As many people learn firsthand, a mosquito bite draws blood and leaves an itchy welt on the victim's skin. Female mosquitoes bite people and animals for the protein in their blood. Male mosquitoes eat only the nectar of flowers and fruits.

⊜ FIGHT FOR LIFE

A major problem in the Everglades is the ongoing contest between native plants and "invaders." These are plants that were brought by people to the Glades—either on purpose, for gardens, or by accident, in the form of pollen. It becomes a problem when nonnative invader plants grow faster and take over land used by native plant species.

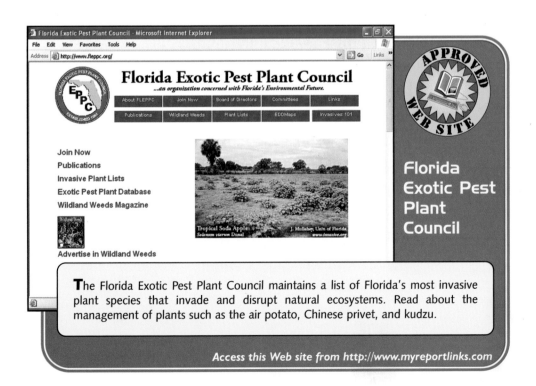

The Florida Exotic Pest Plant Council maintains a list of Florida's most invasive plant species that invade and disrupt natural ecosystems. Read about the management of plants such as the air potato, Chinese privet, and kudzu.

Access this Web site from http://www.myreportlinks.com

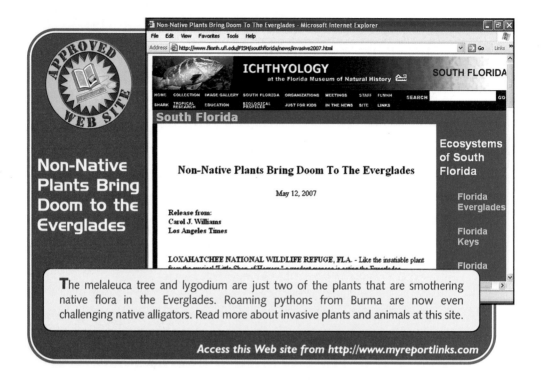

Non-Native Plants Bring Doom to the Everglades

The melaleuca tree and lygodium are just two of the plants that are smothering native flora in the Everglades. Roaming pythons from Burma are now even challenging native alligators. Read more about invasive plants and animals at this site.

Access this Web site from http://www.myreportlinks.com

This takes food away from animals that eat the native plants for survival.

The U.S. Fish and Wildlife Service and ecology groups are working to remove invader plants like the Brazilian pepper to make more room for native plants. They hope that restoring the food chain will help endangered species like nesting birds, as well as native plants such as the morning glory. Everglades National Park is home to over a thousand species of plants. About 20 percent are nonnative invaders.[1]

The manatee is a plant-eater that is in danger from another kind of invader in its habitat: fast-moving speedboats and other motorized watercraft.

Manatees move slowly and cannot swim fast enough to dodge motorboats traveling at high speeds. Some manatees have scars that show where boat propellers have sliced into their skin, and some die from this. Wildlife experts reported that eighty-six manatees were killed by powerboats statewide in 2006.[2]

Marine biologists and zoologists care for injured manatees and help them recover. If all goes well, they are able to release the manatee back into the wild. This is no small task. The large mammal has to be lifted in a special sling and kept wet while being carried by a big truck.

No Wake Zones

The good news is that people are working to prevent manatee accidents. "No Wake Zones" have been set up in rivers, canals, and inlets. There are signs posted wherever manatees have been seen to warn boaters to proceed slowly so that they leave no wake in the water. This is what manatees need to get out of the way in time. Many boaters follow the "No Wake Zone" rules. It will take the work of many people to help save the less than two thousand manatees that are left in Florida.[3]

Everglades National Park rangers recently ran special operations to enforce manatee speed zones. Park rangers in Chokoloskee Bay on the Gulf Coast had to issue twenty-five speeding tickets in two

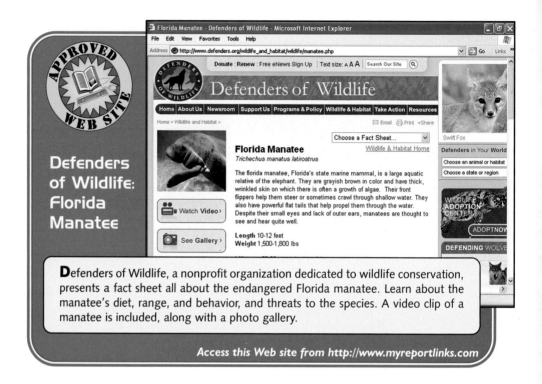

Defenders of Wildlife: Florida Manatee

Defenders of Wildlife, a nonprofit organization dedicated to wildlife conservation, presents a fact sheet all about the endangered Florida manatee. Learn about the manatee's diet, range, and behavior, and threats to the species. A video clip of a manatee is included, along with a photo gallery.

Access this Web site from http://www.myreportlinks.com

days.[4] As more people move to Florida, waterways become more crowded, and so does the coastline. Bass in the rivers, catfish in the marshes, and red snappers, marlins, and sharks in the ocean are all threatened by changes in natural water flows, overfishing, netting, and pollution.

Over the past few decades, the number of Florida panthers has dropped to an all-time low. Everglades National Park staff tries to protect these animals, yet also keep them away from humans. This is for the protection of both panthers and people. Although a panther is unlikely to attack a person, it will go after small pets. Before exploring the Everglades, it is best to learn where

The Florida panther, an endangered subspecies, has dropped to an all-time low. The park strives to protect panthers and also keep them away from humans.

panthers live. Parents should keep pets and small children from wandering off in these areas. Park rangers can provide safety information about panthers and other animals that could be dangerous under certain conditions.

In Everglades National Park, scientists keep watch over panthers by tracking them from airplanes. Or they follow signals from radio collars placed around the big cats' necks. Scientists are in a race with time to save the panther.[5]

Sometimes the only way to protect a species is to keep people out of its habitat altogether. During the

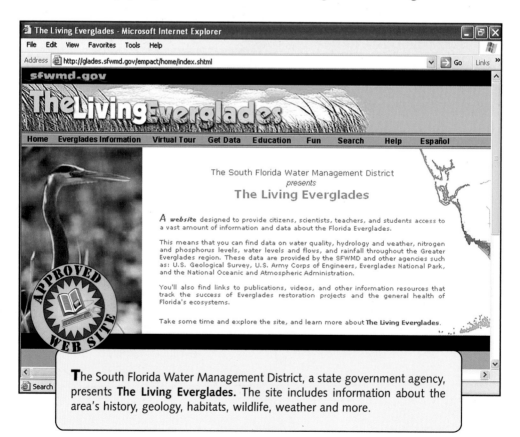

The South Florida Water Management District, a state government agency, presents **The Living Everglades.** The site includes information about the area's history, geology, habitats, wildlife, weather and more.

winter nesting season in December 2006, park staff closed Carl Ross Key to protect roseate spoonbills. Other sites would not have met the needs of these endangered birds, so park staff has closed these areas to the public for now.

⇒ OUT OF BALANCE

Changing the direction of the flow of water over the past century has put the Everglades under major stress. The Everglades is now much smaller than it was at the start of the twentieth century. Everglades National Park staff plays a key role in working to restore the river of grass. In the 1970s and 1980s, the federal and state government enacted laws to clean up and protect the ecosystem. The South Florida Water Management District was the agency responsible for following these laws. It has faced many challenges in recent years.

The agency got into trouble in the late 1980s and into the 1990s. The U.S. government filed a lawsuit on behalf of Everglades National Park and the nearby Loxahatchee National Wildlife Refuge against the state of Florida and the South Florida Water Management District. The United States accused them of allowing toxic runoff—especially phosphorous from farms—into the Everglades. In 1994, an agreement was made and the Florida Everglades Forever Act was formed. It required Florida to restore clean water in damaged areas

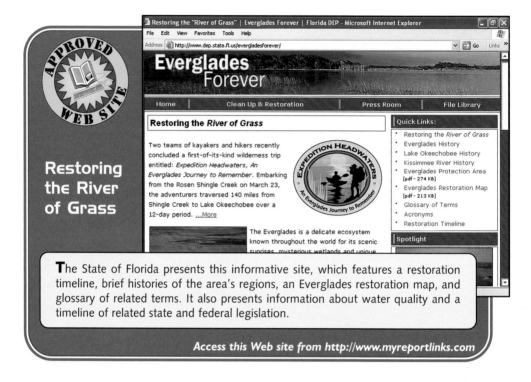

The State of Florida presents this informative site, which features a restoration timeline, brief histories of the area's regions, an Everglades restoration map, and glossary of related terms. It also presents information about water quality and a timeline of related state and federal legislation.

Access this Web site from http://www.myreportlinks.com

and create storm water treatment areas to filter runoff before it reaches the Glades.[6]

Two years later, the U.S. Army Corps of Engineers began to study what it would take to restore the Everglades to its natural balance. The agency presented a plan to the U.S. Congress in 1999. The plan calls for water improvement projects in the Everglades for the next twenty years at a cost of nearly $8 billion.[7]

Today, groups like Friends of the Everglades (founded by the late Marjory Stoneman Douglas) and many other groups are still fighting Florida's sugar farmers over toxins. In 2006, a federal judge ruled that state water managers broke the law by pumping polluted water into Lake Okeechobee. This vast, shallow lake covers 700 square miles (1,813 square kilometers) of southern Florida. Both the Friends of the Everglades and the Miccosukee Tribe worked for this ruling. The court said the South Water Management District broke the federal Clean Water Act. But the state and agency warned that stopping the operations would result in flooding.[8] Answers do not always come easy when it comes to managing the Everglades.

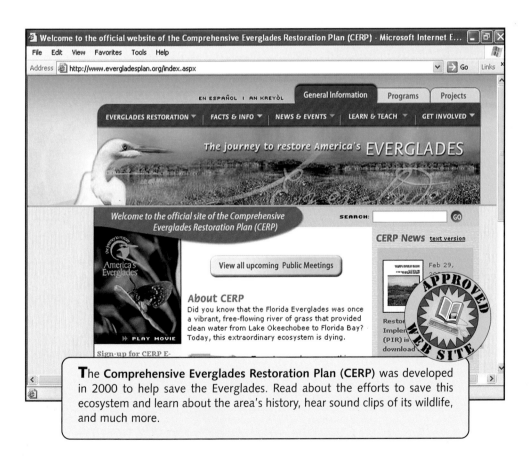

The **Comprehensive Everglades Restoration Plan (CERP)** was developed in 2000 to help save the Everglades. Read about the efforts to save this ecosystem and learn about the area's history, hear sound clips of its wildlife, and much more.

Nearly every day, newspapers present articles about the problems facing this river of saw grass. Today, more people are aware that everyone will have to work together to save this special place. Balancing the needs of Florida's urban centers with those of wildlife will require the efforts of people across the state and Southeast region. They will need to find ways to protect the river of grass from pollution and restore at least some of its natural flow patterns.

⊖ EYE OF THE STORM

Rain is common in south Florida. During the hottest months, thunderstorms bring rain every day. These storms can come up quickly and can seem violent. Everglades' park staff warns tourists to seek shelter if lightning storms come up while they are on walkways.

But these storms do not last long. Lightning strikes dried brush, and this can mean the start of a wildfire. Park staff keeps watch for fires throughout the storm season. In the spring of 2007, wildfires spread down from Georgia and destroyed thousands of acres in northern Florida. As far south as Orlando, the air was thick with a smoky haze for many days.

Yet fires can be good for the Everglades system. Some of the pine trees and other plants in the area are able to withstand the flames, while other plants cannot. When they burn up, it allows sunshine to get through and clears the way for pines and other plants to grow.

Hurricanes are also natural events and common in south Florida. One of the biggest in modern times was Hurricane Andrew, which moved over Florida's southeast, central and Gulf Coasts in 1992. It killed forty people and destroyed homes and property totaling billions of dollars. It left thousands of people homeless and without food or clean water for weeks. People had to live in tents and emergency shelters for months afterward.

➲ INTENSE AND DESTRUCTIVE HURRICANES

Like Hurricane Andrew, Hurricane San Felipe Segundo was a Category 5 hurricane. Scientists rate hurricanes from 1 to 5 according to the "Saffir-Simpson scale." The rating is based on the storm's intensity; a Category 5 hurricane has winds greater than 155 miles per hour. Hurricane San Felipe Segundo was also called the Okee-chobee Hurricane. In 1928, it struck Puerto Rico and the Caribbean and then went on to hit West Palm Beach on Florida's Atlantic Coast. It crossed over Lake Okeechobee in its path.

The storm surge from the lake breached the dike and flooded hundreds of square miles. In some places, the water rose as high as 20 feet (6.1 meters). The flood killed thousands of people,

An aerial view of damage done by Hurricane Andrew in South Dade County, Florida.

many of them farmworkers.[9] Survivors had to hang on to rooftops to escape rising floodwaters. Alligators and snakes swam around them. Animals scrambled on top of buildings alongside people to escape the rising water.

A hurricane can destroy a town. Trees snap with the force of high winds. Walls cave in and roofs tumble down to the ground. But the winds blow away dried brush and make room for other plants to spring to life in the sunshine that follows.

➡ THE EYE OF THE STORM

In the days before a hurricane, the sky is blue with no signs of the raging storm to come. Then suddenly the winds pick up as the storm approaches. After many hours, what is called the "eye" of the hurricane passes overhead. The sky opens up, the sun bursts through, and for about fifteen to twenty minutes, it seems as though the worst is over.

But this is actually just the first half of the storm. The eye is a hole in the middle of the hurricane. Soon the remainder of the storm, or "wall," follows. Within seconds, it is back to the roaring sound of mighty winds and the crack of breaking trees.

It is important that people in Florida stay equipped with emergency supplies, because there is a chance of a hurricane each summer. Even visitors should keep up with local weather reports. Many residents board up windows when a hurricane is approaching. Others leave the area.

Sometimes police must coax people out of their homes when the outlook for an approaching storm is very bad. Many of these people stay in schools or other shelters until the storm passes. Even though a new, higher dike has been built around Lake Okeechobee since the big hurricane eighty years ago, some locals still move to high ground when a hurricane threatens.

Chapter 6

Some visitors to the park enjoy gliding through its cool mangrove forests in a kayak.

Cruise the Swamp and Sea

A visit to Everglades National Park can mean many things. It may mean cruising on a boat around the southern tip of Florida, then stopping at one of the tropical islands called the Keys. It can mean scuba or snorkel diving above coral reef gardens in the Biscayne and John Pennekamp bays. It can mean gathering shells and watching a sunset on the Gulf of Mexico, or camping on a sandy beach.

It may also mean learning more about Florida's wildlife. For example, each year, visitors cheer on turtles as they return to the sea. South Florida has 90 percent of the sea turtle nesting sites in the United States. Federal and state governments have been awarding money to groups to help these animals. People protect the turtles while they nest during summer.[1]

Yet there are other ways to enjoy sea life without getting wet—or full of sand. Many visitors to Biscayne National Park, just south of the Everglades, board a glass-bottomed boat. This setup lets people get a good look at tropical fish, marine mammals like dolphins, and also sea turtles from above as the boat glides over the park's coral reef.

Guided tours are available at a price most people can afford. Since the available seats on these boats fill up fast, visitors should call ahead.[2]

WALK, SKIP—OR FLOAT

Whether you are driving east to west on "Alligator Alley" (Interstate-75) through the Big Cypress National Preserve, or north to south on the Tamiami Trail (U.S. Highway 41), you will see license plates with pictures of endangered animals on them. Residents of Florida can buy special license plates for their cars that portray sea turtles, panthers, manatees, large mouth bass, or other species in danger of dying out. This is one way to help people remember to slow down and watch for animals while driving. They are fun to look at, and the money people pay for the plates is used by Florida scientists for wildlife research.

Some visitors enjoy gliding in a kayak or canoe through cool mangrove forests on the coast. The Gulf Coast Visitor Center is the gateway to Ten Thousand Islands, a mangrove forest, and waterways that lead to the Florida Bay. After a long day of paddling, there are restaurants, stores, motels, and campgrounds nearby.

Those in search of a more rugged wilderness experience can camp in the Ten Thousand Island

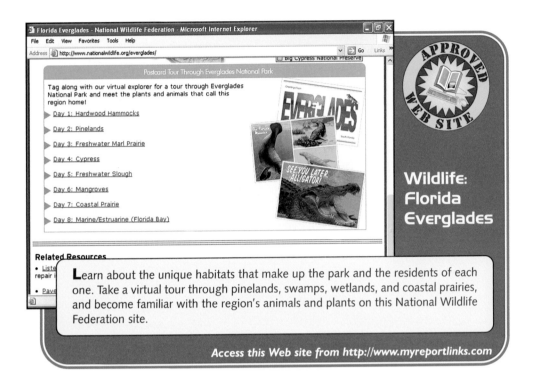

Florida Everglades - National Wildlife Federation - Microsoft Internet Explorer

File   Edit   View   Favorites   Tools   Help

Address http://www.nationalwildlife.org/everglades/   Go   Links

Big Cypress National Preserve

Postcard Tour Through Everglades National Park

Tag along with our virtual explorer for a tour through Everglades
National Park and meet the plants and animals that call this
region home!

Day 1: Hardwood Hammocks

Day 2: Pinelands

Day 3: Freshwater Marl Prairie

Day 4: Cypress

Day 5: Freshwater Slough

Day 6: Mangroves

Day 7: Coastal Prairie

Day 8: Marine/Estruarine (Florida Bay)

Related Resources

• Liste
repair i

• Pave

**Wildlife:
Florida
Everglades**

Learn about the unique habitats that make up the park and the residents of each
one. Take a virtual tour through pinelands, swamps, wetlands, and coastal prairies,
and become familiar with the region's animals and plants on this National Wildlife
Federation site.

Access this Web site from http://www.myreportlinks.com

National Wildlife Refuge on Florida's Gulf Coast.
This refuge is part of the largest mangrove forest
in North America. Florida's white, black, and red
mangroves are tropical, so they need warm temperatures to survive. There are also mangrove
forests near Cape Canaveral on Florida's Atlantic
Coast. Black mangroves grow in the northern part
of Florida. Many people enjoy fishing in these
calm, watery mazes.

Some people like to take in the scenery at a
slower pace, so they hike on boardwalks through
Everglades marshes. In the heart of the saw grass
is the Shark Valley Visitor Center. There are guided
tours and bicycle rentals available here. Visitors

▲ The Anhinga Trail is a popular hiking route located near the Royal Palm Visitor Center. Here it passes through a saw grass marsh in Taylor Slough.

can also buy film, insect repellent, hats, snacks, drinks, and other items at the center. Many Everglades tourist shops sell these items.

There are hiking trails in the southern part of the park that are paved or have been made into wooden boardwalks. One is the Anhinga Trail, which loops through a saw grass marsh in Taylor Slough. A slough (pronounced "slew") is like a pond with a slow current. This trail is near the Royal Palm Visitor Center. Just north of this site is the Ernest Coe Visitor Center, which is open year-round. It has displays and films on the Everglades's science and history, and was named for one of the park's founders.

On Long Pine Key to the west is a trail that stretches through a pine forest. Here, wildflowers and ferns are underfoot. Pinelands Trail has a boardwalk that leads to an observation tower. From the tower, visitors can view vast grassy waters and a large cypress dome.

Another trail to the west is a boardwalk that begins on low ground and leads to Mahogany Hammock on higher ground. Wheelchairs can

▽ *One of the many boardwalk trails available to visitors of the park.*

Airboats float near the water's surface. Because they can be very loud and disturb wildlife, they are not allowed within the park's borders. But specially made airboats with quiet motors are available for "Eco Tours" in the Everglades.

move on many of these boardwalk trails. The park also has bicycle paths. Pets are not allowed on park trails, however. There are many reasons for this rule. Pets can harm the ecosystem and get in the way of other people and animals. They also attract alligators.

South of this hammock trail is the Flamingo Visitor Center Campground. Everyone who camps in Everglades National Park needs a permit. There are boat ramps near the center, as well as hiking trails. Parts of the center are currently closed due to damage caused by Hurricanes Katrina and Wilma in 2005. It is a good idea to call before a visit to check on the present state of the park.

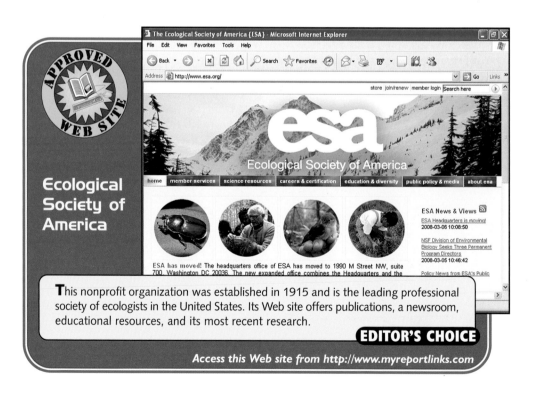

Ecological Society of America

This nonprofit organization was established in 1915 and is the leading professional society of ecologists in the United States. Its Web site offers publications, a newsroom, educational resources, and its most recent research.

EDITOR'S CHOICE

Access this Web site from http://www.myreportlinks.com

➔ BEST BY BOAT

Everglades National Park is best traveled by boat. There are many possible paths and waterways to explore. In the Florida Bay, there are dozens of keys, which are small islands. But boating in the Everglades, either in the swamp or in the sea, is for people who know what they are doing. There are long banks of mud and sea grass, oyster reefs, and sandbars, all of which could strand a boat. Shallow areas are not always marked. Drivers must truly act as boat captains. They must look for signs of bad weather and read ocean charts to track the tides.

For many people, travel in the Everglades means zipping around in an airboat at high speed. Tours launch from spots near the park, and some companies will even pick up visitors from their hotels. Airboats float near the top of the water's surface and do not cause much drag as they move over water. They are powered by a large propeller, which looks like a fan, in back. But as mentioned in chapter 1, airboat motors can be loud. Drivers and riders often wear earplugs or other headgear to muffle the sound.

Public airboats are not allowed within the borders of Everglades National Park. This is to ensure that the wetlands inside the park remain a quiet place for both people and wildlife. However, private companies do offer guided airboat rides to tourists in certain locations, such as along the Tamiami Trail or around Everglades City. Other types of boat (and tram) tours are run within the park.

People who are most excited about viewing or photographing wildlife in Everglades National Park can ride airboats with specially made "quiet" motors. These airboat drivers host rides called Eco Tours. The "Eco" stands for the tour's focus on the Everglades natural ecosystem. The tours are led by drivers who know where to spot wildlife and can talk about native plants and animals. They have become more popular in recent years as more people learn about the problems faced by the Everglades.

Those who tour the area of the Everglades may see a slimy, yellowish-green coating on the water. This is algae, a plant that forms a "mat" that filters the water and provides food for insects, snails, and shrimp. It is the first part of a long food chain of plants and animals in the Everglades. Sometimes visitors mistake the algae as having formed because of pollution. But it is the other way around; pollution is a threat to the algae.

⇨ ALLIGATOR WRESTLING

Beef cattle ranches surround Lake Okeechobee, and there are dairies to the south. Living alongside these ranches are Florida's modern-day American Indians. Both groups are skilled at riding horses, roping steers, and performing other activities found in most American-style rodeos.

But Everglades's rodeos offer visitors a unique twist—alligator wrestling for sport. The contest between a wrestler and an alligator is often very short. Wrestlers know a special way to make the alligator lie down. These events are held in small stadiums. Fans can cheer on their favorite cowboy or wrestler from the stands. They can sip fresh fruit drinks or sweetened iced tea simmered in the heat of the sun.

SUNSHINE STATE CUISINE

Of course, a glass of orange, grapefruit, or lime juice sweetened with raw sugar is always a welcome treat in the Sunshine State. These drinks go well with snacks such as roasted alligator bits dipped in barbecue sauce, turtle stew, grilled or boiled shrimp, breaded frog legs, or conch fritters. Both restaurants and roadside stands sell dishes that meet the needs of those at the top of the Everglades food chain—humans!

Many Florida foods are shipped to other parts of America for sale. The leading port in Florida is in the city of Tampa, northwest of the Everglades.[3] Shrimp, lobsters, and scallops bring in the most money. Catfish is a favorite freshwater catch. Saltwater fish such as grouper, mackerel, and red snapper are also popular.

Top restaurant and hotel chefs throughout Florida will cook up special recipes made from these

Sunset at the J. N. "Ding" Darling National Wildlife Refuge on Sanibel Island, a barrier island just west of the park.

foods for guests. Chewy conch fritters, shellfish that are breaded, deep-fried, then dipped in a tangy sauce, are popular throughout Florida and in the Keys. The state is also famous for its Key lime pie, a creamy, sweet-and-sour dessert. On hot days, it can be served frozen so that it tastes more like an ice cream treat. These dishes are served in Florida's "southern" kitchens.

SANIBEL ISLAND'S SHELLS AND BIRDS

Sanibel Island is a barrier island off the Gulf Coast just west of Everglades National Park. It is known for the billions of colorful seashells that wash up on its beaches. In some spots on the island, the layer of shells rises up to the height of a grown man's knees! Shops around the island display necklaces, picture frames, and hundreds of other items made from seashells. Many families rent hotel rooms or buy vacation homes here. Children enjoy building sand castles on its beaches.

The J. N. "Ding" Darling National Wildlife Refuge is also on Sanibel Island. It is a safe home for migratory birds, and the refuge has a wildlife viewing roadway and education center. Visitors can begin their day by touring the subtropical mangroves and wetlands in the refuge by bicycle. Then they can stroll along the warm waters of the Gulf of Mexico in the afternoon.

Key West is the last of a string of islands south of the Florida Bay. It is part of a chain of islands that offers popular vacation spots. Some of these islands are remote, while others have been built up to meet the needs of tourists. There is a ranger station on Key Largo, the largest of these. West of the island of Key West is a small chain of seven islands that are now Dry Tortugas Island National Park.

The Dry Tortugas were found by Spanish explorers in the sixteenth century. Coral reefs around these islands caused many shipwrecks. Some say pirates' treasure is buried here. Sea turtles that lived among the islands became food for sailors and pirates who traveled to them. But there

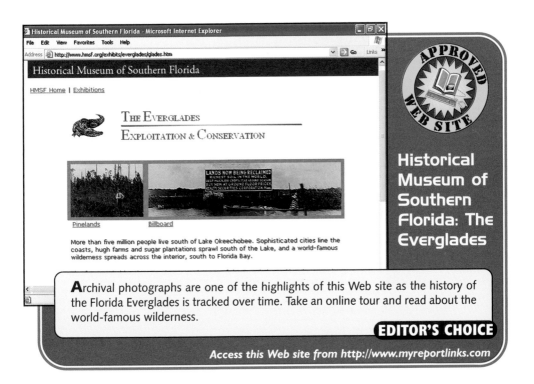

Historical Museum of Southern Florida: The Everglades

Archival photographs are one of the highlights of this Web site as the history of the Florida Everglades is tracked over time. Take an online tour and read about the world-famous wilderness.

EDITOR'S CHOICE

Access this Web site from http://www.myreportlinks.com

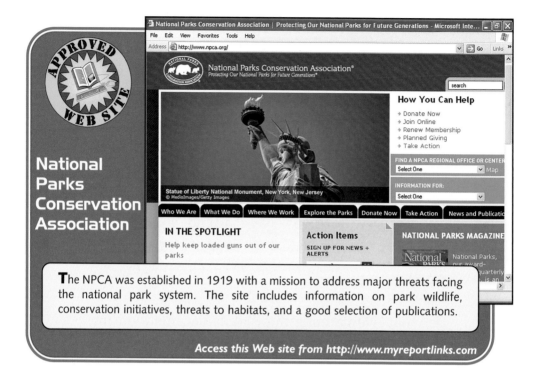

National Parks Conservation Association

The NPCA was established in 1919 with a mission to address major threats facing the national park system. The site includes information on park wildlife, conservation initiatives, threats to habitats, and a good selection of publications.

Access this Web site from http://www.myreportlinks.com

is no freshwater on these islands. This is how they came to be named "Dry," while the word Tortugas is old Spanish for "turtles." Nearly all who travel here come by boat.

In the early 1800s, the U.S. military planned to build a fort on the island. But the plan to build what would have been Fort Jefferson was never finished. New weapons, such as the rifle cannon, made it less important to have a fort in the sea.[4]

But the coral reef, sea life, and nesting birds made this place ideal as a wildlife refuge. In 1935, President Franklin D. Roosevelt made Fort Jefferson a national monument. In 1992, the islands became the Dry Tortugas National Park.

Traveling by boat to tiny islands, or zooming over miles of saw grass, is all part of life in south Florida and the Everglades. Florida officially became the twenty-seventh U.S. state on March 3, 1845. Its state flag is white with a colorful crest that shows both land and water in the center. It also has a bold, red "X" so that it would not look like a white surrender flag.[5]

This flag reflects the spirit of Florida's founders. These men and women had visions for a better future; they did not give up when things got tough. Native Seminoles fought to keep their homeland and won. Pioneers settled Florida and made it a world-famous vacation spot. People are still moving to Florida to enjoy its natural beauty, economy, and the cheery "Sunshine State" lifestyle. Perhaps this same spirit of hope for the future will save Everglades National Park in the years to come.

Report Links

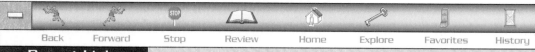

The Internet sites described below can be accessed at http://www.myreportlinks.com

▶**National Park Service: Everglades National Park**
Editor's Choice This National Park Service site provides a very good overview of the park.

▶**Water's Journey: Everglades**
Editor's Choice This guide is an online companion to a PBS series.

▶**Ecological Society of America**
Editor's Choice Conservation and preservation of ecological sites are the goals of this association.

▶**Historical Museum of Southern Florida: The Everglades**
Editor's Choice The museum's online exhibition explores this unique tropical region.

▶**Comprehensive Everglades Restoration Plan (CERP)**
Editor's Choice Learn about the effort to save the Florida Everglades.

▶**The Nature Conservancy**
Editor's Choice This conservation organization works to preserve wildlife and conserve habitats.

▶**Andrew Jackson (1767–1845)**
The Miller Center of Public Affairs presents a comprehensive collection of material on U.S. presidents.

▶**Defenders of Wildlife: Florida Manatee**
This nonprofit organization's site provides interesting facts about the Florida manatee.

▶**Everglades**
This Web site provides information about the diverse plant and animal life of the Everglades.

▶**Everglades Digital Library**
View an online exhibition about the Everglades.

▶**The Everglades in the Time of Marjory Stoneman Douglas**
These photographs from the Florida Memory Project's collection document the Everglades.

▶**The Evolution of the Conservation Movement, 1850–1920**
This collection includes photographs and manuscripts about the movement to conserve our heritage.

▶**Exploring the Environment: Florida Everglades**
Learn about the Everglades on this site.

▶**Florida Exotic Pest Plant Council**
For information on invasive plants in Florida, visit this Web site.

▶**Henry Morrison Flagler Museum**
Learn about the Gilded Age and Henry Flagler on this Web site.

Report Links

The Internet sites described below can be accessed at
http://www.myreportlinks.com

▶**History of Audubon of Florida**
This is a historical time line for Audubon of Florida.

▶**The Living Everglades**
Find detailed information about the Everglades on this site.

▶**Marjory Stoneman Douglas: Defender of the Everglades**
This Friends of the Everglades Web site presents a biography of Marjory Stoneman Douglas.

▶**National Invasive Species Information Center**
This is a government gateway to invasive species information.

▶**National Parks Conservation Association**
The mission of this environmental nonprofit is to protect and preserve America's national parks.

▶**Native Aquatic and Wetland Plants in Florida**
The Center for Aquatic and Invasive Plants presents information on plant management.

▶**Non-Native Plants Bring Doom to the Everglades**
This *Los Angeles Times* article focuses on invasive plants in the national park.

▶**Oh, Ranger!: Everglades National Park**
An information guide for the Everglades.

▶**Rebellion: John Horse and the Black Seminoles, the First Black Rebels to Beat American Slavery**
This Web documentary includes slide shows, interactive maps, and beautiful illustrations.

▶**Reclaiming the Everglades: South Florida's Natural History 1884–1934**
The Library of Congress presents a collection of materials from three South Florida libraries.

▶**Restoring the River of Grass**
This State of Florida Web site provides information about restoring the Everglades.

▶**Reviving the River of Grass**
This extensive *Audubon* magazine article offers information on restoration plans for the park.

▶**Seminoles and Slaves: Florida's Freedom Seekers**
This article focuses on the Seminole Wars.

▶**Threats to Florida's Biodiversity**
Saving the natural habitats of Florida is the focus of this article.

▶**Wildlife: Florida Everglades**
Take an online tour of the Everglades on this site.

agency—A government division.

bedrock—Solid rock beneath soil.

boardwalk—A walkway made of planks of wood along a beach.

brackish—Somewhat salty.

breach—To break or violate.

conservation—Protection of a natural resource.

estuary—Water passage where the ocean tide meets a river's current.

evaporation—The process by which water turns from its liquid form into vapor.

hammocks—High ground with rich soil that is densely wooded.

mangroves—Tropical coastal trees or shrubs with extended root systems.

marshes—Soft wet land that often hosts grasses.

native—Grown or originating in a particular place; local.

nonnative—Refers to a plant or animal species that originated in a part of the world other than where it currently lives.

Pangaea—The supercontinent (meaning "all lands" in Greek) thought to have broken up some 225-200 million years ago. It eventually fragmented into the continents we know today.

prehistoric—Ancient time period before written history.

propeller—A device with a central hub and blades used to propel a vehicle.

scuba—<u>S</u>elf-<u>c</u>ontained <u>u</u>nderwater <u>b</u>reathing <u>a</u>pparatus.

service trades—In general, occupations that involve attending to the needs or requests of people.

slough—A place of deep muddy "backwater" formed by a creek or a river inlet in a marsh or a tide flat.

snorkel—A tube for air intake and exhaust that enables a swimmer to stay beneath the water's surface.

storm surge—The quick rise and fall of the ocean on the coastline as the result of a storm.

wake—The track left by a moving body in water.

wetlands—Land alternately covered with shallow water and moisture-rich soil.

Chapter 1. World-Famous "River of Grass"

1. National Oceanic & Atmospheric Administration's National Severe Storms Laboratory, "A Severe Weather Primer: Questions & Answers About Lightning," National Weather Center-Norman, OK, December 4, 2007, <http://www.nssl.noaa.gov/primer/lightning/ltg_climatology.html> (January 21, 2008).

2. Microsoft Encarta® Online Encyclopedia 2007, "Reptile," VI. *Evolution,* 1997–2007, <http://encarta.msn.com/encyclopedia_761579044_3/Reptile.html> (January 31, 2008).

3. National Park Service, "Endangered Species," *Everglades National Park,* October 13, 1999, <http://www.nps.gov/archive/ever/eco/danger.htm> (January 19, 2008).

4. National Park Service, "Species Loss," *Everglades National Park,"* November 10, 1997, <http://www.nps.gov/archive/ever/eco/spploss.htm> (January 31, 2008).

5. National Park Service, FAQ: Big Cypress National Preserve, n.d., <www.nps.gov/archive/bicy/faqs.htm> (January 31, 2008).

6. National Park Service, "Flamingo Visitor Center," *Everglades National Park,* November 8, 2007, <www.nps.gov/ever/planyourvisit/flamdirections.htm> (January 31, 2008).

7. The Olympian-Outdoors column, "Fish awesome sights in Jurassic Park," Chester Allen, April 20, 2007, <www.TheOlympian.com/107/story/85283.html> (January 21, 2008).

8. Marjory Stoneman Douglas, *The Everglades: River of Grass* (New York: Rinehart & Company, 1947), pp. 382–385.

9. Public Broadcasting Service television series underwritten by New York Life Insurance Company &

produced by Thirteen/WNET-New York, "Slavery and the Making of America," aired February 9 and February 16, 2004, <http://www.slaveryinamerica.org/scripts/sia/glossary.cgi> (January 20, 2008).

10. United States Census Bureau, American Fact Finder, 2006, "Florida: Selected Economic Characteristics," <http://factfinder.census.gov> (January 21, 2008).

Chapter 2. Never Surrendered

1. Marjory Stoneman Douglas, *The Everglades: River of Grass* (New York: Rinehart & Company, 1947), pp. 7–9

2. Ibid.

3. Travel Features Syndicate, "In St. Augustine, City of 'Oldests' Experience History, Nature Anew," 2007, <http://www.travelwritersmagazine.com/TravelFeaturesSyndicate/St.Augustine-Attractions.html> (January 20, 2008).

4. Ibid.

5. University of Florida, Institute of Food and Agricultural Sciences (UF/IFAS), "Florida's Geological History," May 2005, <http://edis.ifas.ufl.edu/UW208> (January 20, 2008).

6. Ibid.

7. Seminole Tribe of Florida, "A Legendary Storyteller—Betty Mae Jumper," 2004, <http://www.seminoletribe.com/culture/storyteller.shtml> (January 20, 2008).

8. Wilfred T. Neill, *Florida's Seminole Indians* (St. Petersburg, Fla.: Great Outdoors Publishing Co., 1956), pp. 8–9.

Chapter 3. Guardians of the Saw Grass

1. Everglades Information Network Digital Library/Florida International University, n.d., <http://everglades.fiu.edu/reclaim/bios/flagler.htm> (January 20, 2008).

2. National Park Service, "Park Establishment: South Florida's Watery Wilderness Park Nears 50," January 6, 1999, <http://www.nps.gov/archive/ever/eco/nordeen.htm> (January 21, 2008).

3. Ibid.

4. National Park Service, "Ernest F. Coe—Father of the Everglades," *Everglades National Park,* June 1, 1999, <http://www.nps.gov/archive/ever/eco/coe.htm> (January 21, 2008).

5. National Park Service, "Marjory Stoneman Douglas," Everglades National Park, March 3, 2000, <http://www.nps.gov/archive/ever/eco/marjory.htm> (January 21, 2008).

6. Marjory Stoneman Douglas, *The Everglades: River of Grass* (New York: Rinehart & Company, 1947), p. 5.

Chapter 4. Mangroves and Mermaids

1. Encyclopædia Britannica Online: "Limpkin," n.d., <http://www.britannica.com/eb/article-9048325/limpkin> (January 20, 2008).

2. National Geographic Adventures: "Sandhill Crane," National Geographic Society, 1996–2008, <http://www.nationalgeographic.com/animals/birds/sandhill-crane.html> (January 20, 2008).

3. Australian Museum Online, "Orb Weaving Spiders," 2003, <http://www.amonline.net.au/factsheets/orb_weaving_spiders.htm> (January 20, 2008).

4. State of Florida, *MyFWC.com: Wildlife Alert! Information, 1999–2006* <http://www.panther.state.fl.us> (January 20, 2008).

5. U.S. Fish & Wildlife Service, "National Key Deer Refuge," *Fact Sheet,* n.d., <http://www.fws.gov /nationalkeydeer/> (January 20, 2008).

6. Doreen Cubie, "Are These Kites Headed For A Fall?" *National Wildlife,* vol. 45, no. 1, Dec./Jan. 2007 <http://www.nwf.org/nationalwildlife/article.cfm? issueID=112&articleID=1419> (January 31, 2008).

7. Dawn Henthorn, "The Seven Wonders of Florida: Florida's Coral Reefs," *FlaUSA.com, About.com,* 2008, <http://goflorida.about.com/od/allaboutflorida /ss/7wonders_3.htm> (January 20, 2008).

Chapter 5. Food Chain Invaders and Other Threats

1. National Park Service, "Flamingo Visitor Center," *Everglades National Park,* November 8, 2007, <http://www.nps.gov/ever/planyourvisit/flamdirections .htm> (January 13, 2008).

2. National Park Service, "Manatee Speed Zone Enforcement in Chokoloskee Bay," *Everglades National Park,* March 2, 2007, <http://www.nps.gov/ever /parknews/chokoloskeebay.htm> (January 21, 2008).

3. Save The Manatee Club, Synoptic Surveys 1991–2006, <http://www.savethemanatee.org /population4a.htm> (January 30, 2008).

4. National Park Service, "Manatee Speed Zone Enforcement in Chokoloskee Bay."

5. University of Florida, Institute of Food and Agricultural Sciences (UF/IFAS) for the People of the State of Florida, n.d., <http://edis.ifas.ufl.edu/ UW209> (January 31, 2008).

6. National Park Service, "Evolution of Ecosystem Restoration Efforts," *Everglades National Park,* March 3, 2000, <http://www.nps.gov/archive/ever/eco/restore .htm> (January 20, 2008).

7. Ibid.

8. Curt Anderson, the Associated Press, "Federal

judge rules water managers illegally pumped dirty water into Lake O," December 12, 2006, *Friends of the Everglades Web site*, <http://www.everglades.org/news121206.html> (January 20, 2008).

9. Liz Doup, "1928 Okeechobee—The Night 2,000 Died," September 11, 1998, *Florida Sun-Sentinel Online 2008*, <http://www.sun-sentinel.com/news/weather/hurricane/sfl-1928-hurricane,0,2734526.story> (January 30, 2008).

Chapter 6. Cruise the Swamp and Sea

1. Florida Environment Radio Programs, "Sea Turtles—Tending the Nest," n.d., <http://www.floridaenvironment.com/programs/fe00717.htm> (January 30, 2008).

2. National Park Service, "Biscayne Guided Tours," *Biscayne National Park,* December 16, 2007, <http://www.nps.gov/biscplanyourvisit/guidedtours.htm> (January 30, 2008).

3. Richard Wainio, Port Director and Chief Executive Officer, Tampa Port Authority, "State of the Port Address," December 12, 2007, <http://www.tampaport.com/subpage.asp?mavid=0&id=58> (January 30, 2008).

4. National Park Service, "Dry Tortugas National Park: History and Culture," *Dry Tortugas National Park* September 13, 2007 <http://www.nps.gov/drto/historyculture/index.htm> (January 30, 2008).

5. State of Florida, "Florida's State Symbols," *Cultural and Historical Information Programs,* n.d., <www.flheritage.com/facts/symbols/symbol.cfm?page=1&id=1> (January 31, 2008).

Ake, Anne. *Everglades: An Ecosystem Facing Choices and Challenges*. Sarasota, Fla.: Pineapple Press, 2007.

Burgan, Michael. *The Spanish Conquest of America*. New York: Chelsea House, 2007.

Cannavale, Matthew C. *Voices from Colonial America: Florida, 1513-1821*. Washington, D.C.: National Geographic, 2006.

Davenport, John C. *Juan Ponce de León and His Lands of Discovery*. Philadelphia: Chelsea House, 2006.

Fletcher, Marty and Glenn Scherer. *The Florida Panther: Help Save This Endangered Species!* Berkeley Heights, N.J.: MyReportLinks.com Books, 2006.

Hart, Joyce and Perry Chang. *Florida*. New York: Marshall Cavendish Benchmark, 2007.

Hubbard, Janet. *Hernando de Soto and His Expeditions Across the Americas*. Philadelphia: Chelsea House, 2006.

Lynch, Wayne. *The Everglades*. Minnetonka, Minn.: NorthWord Books for Young Readers, 2007.

Snyder, Trish. *Alligator & Crocodile Rescue: Changing the Future For Endangered Wildlife*. Buffalo: Firefly Books, 2006.

Treaster, Joseph B. *Hurricane Force: In the Path of America's Deadliest Storms*. Boston: Kingfisher, 2007.

Wilcox, Charlotte. *The Seminoles*. Minneapolis: Lerner Publications Co., 2007.